Marx

ALSO AVAILABLE FROM BLOOMSBURY

Marx:
An Introduction

Michel Henry

Foreword by Frédéric Seyler
Translated by Kristien Justaert

BLOOMSBURY ACADEMIC
LONDON • NEW YORK • OXFORD • NEW DELHI • SYDNEY

BLOOMSBURY ACADEMIC
Bloomsbury Publishing Plc
50 Bedford Square, London, WC1B 3DP, UK
1385 Broadway, New York, NY 10018, USA

BLOOMSBURY, BLOOMSBURY ACADEMIC and the Diana logo are
trademarks of Bloomsbury Publishing Plc

First published as Le socialisme selon Marx, Michel Henry © Éditions
Sulliver, 2008

English translation © Bloomsbury Publishing Plc, 2019

Cover design: Catherine Wood

A catalogue record for this book is available from the British Library.

A catalogue record for this book is available from the Library of Congress.

ISBN: HB: 978-1-4742-6942-1
PB: 978-1-4742-7778-5
ePDF: 978-1-4742-6943-8
ePub: 978-1-4742-6944-5

Typeset by Newgen KnowledgeWorks Pvt. Ltd., Chennai, India
Printed and bound in Great Britain

To find out more about our authors and books visit www.bloomsbury.com
and sign up for our newsletters.

Contents

Foreword

Michel Henry's approach with regard to political economy – that is, first and foremost with regard to Marx – can perhaps be best summarized with the idea that the economy, as such, must always be subordinated to living subjectivity. In other words, *life* as fundamental and *non*-economic reality is the 'frame' outside of which economic reality has, precisely, no reality. Such is the requisite for philosophy: to think of the economic only with a view on life, since it is only life, phenomenologically understood as the ultimate power of *manifestation*, that makes economics intelligible, not vice versa. From this standpoint – the standpoint of the radical phenomenology of life inaugurated by Henry – Marxism cannot be seen otherwise than as a gigantic misinterpretation of Marx insofar as it radically reverses the aforementioned order and, on the contrary, subordinates life to what it sees as its fundamental determination: economic reality. According to Henry, what Marxism does not see is that the economic is only an *un*real and fantasized *double* of reality, that is, of life itself.

In order to understand this assertion fully, we have to follow Henry's reading of Marx as a *genealogy* of the economic.

Economic 'reality' essentially originates in the exchange of use values (*Gebrauchswerte*) that subsequently become exchange values (*Tauschwerte*). But how is this exchange possible? That is, how shall we measure the value of different products of human labour, which is – ultimately – *individual* labour? 'In the exchange, two use values, two products are put in each other's presence. They have absolutely nothing in common. On the one hand, it concerns a certain quantity of linen, on the other hand a certain quantity of wheat or metal, or anything one would want. How can we establish an equality between all these products?' (25).[1] The only solution, it seems, is to adopt an *objective* scale that measures labour and to apply this measurement to the product of labour as exchange value. The problem with such a process is, however, that it distorts the essence of labour: it is not real labour that it measures, but only its *representation*. As a principle, a representation is always exterior to what it represents. The representation of labour thus becomes, on the one hand, the instrument of its quantitative and qualitative determination. On the other hand, real labour, or labour as real, is profoundly alien to representation. Its reality is, on the contrary, *subjective*, rooted in individual effort or, to speak using a key concept of Henry's phenomenology, *immanent*. Representations are only the attempted, yet as such impossible, translation of radically subjective affectivity into the language of the world: the language of objects and numbers that *transcend* living praxis, interior and invisible. Economics therefore implies a derealization of labour, transforming it into represented labour, that is, into an unreal double of what is, on the contrary, lived through or *épreuve*: 'Marx's thesis is that economics is only an abstraction. Economic reality is not the true, ultimate reality, but presupposes this reality and refers to it. This fundamental reality that grounds economics and ultimately determines it, is the individual subjective life' (19).

Economic 'realities' are thus, and in principle, literally the result of a departure from reality – the result of a process of '*alienation*'. They are the consequence of an abstraction that substitutes the general for the singular, the social for the individual or, in short, the ideal (in the sense of belonging to ideality and representation) for the real. However, as Henry acknowledges, there is no alternative to abstraction and the measurement of labour if products are to be exchanged. Rather, his critique targets the fact that the process of abstraction is not *recognized* for what it is, namely, as the process by which an unreal double of real labour is created. Unrecognized, such a process leads to the disastrous assumption that the abstract *is* the real. This unmasking of a fundamental confusion between living subjectivity and its objective 'equivalents' is what Henry identifies at the heart of the Marxian critique of political economy. In Henry's reading, Marx has clearly established that labour, as subjective, radically escapes objectifying determinations, both qualitative and quantitative.

> For Marx, *the* labour doesn't exist. There are only concrete, individual, determined, subjective, and qualitatively different labour processes . . . For it is not only the diverse kinds of labour that are different. The 'same' work, done by two different individuals, is not the 'same' . . . The time of their

activity is not the same: their existences cannot be exchanged, they are not comparable and the real labour, its subjective temporality, a particular mode of a particular existence, is not exchangeable either. (26)

Hence, the following paradox: an objective determination of labour seems as necessary (as a condition of possibility for exchange) as it is impossible (due to the essential difference between reality and the representation of reality). Hence, also, Henry's solution: real labour is not to be confused with labour as represented, the latter being nothing but a convenient *fiction*, artificially created out of socio-economic necessity. It is noteworthy that, as Henry stresses in his 1987 essay *Barbarism*, the confusion between immanent life and its abstract representation is an essential characteristic of scientism. There, scientism is defined by the *ontological* claim that empirical–mathematical methods and their objects alone constitute an adequate account of reality; even more, that reality *is*, ultimately, constituted by what empirical sciences define as objects, laws and so on. Scientism is not science, though, but an ideology that, according to Henry, has dominated modern and contemporary times and has led to a new form of barbarism, that is, to the negation of life as subjective and immanent.

If we now return to the specific realm of economics, money, for instance, is analysed as doubling the unreality pertaining to the representation of labour. Subjective labour first becomes reified in exchange value, to which in turn a money equivalent is assigned that is independent of the product. Money is the abstract

form given to value, the *representation of a representation*, thus
departing even further from real labour.

For Henry, the idea that money – that is, capital – could
generate value by itself can arise only out of a failure to recognize
the transcendental genesis of money as a representation of a
representation (of labour). Without the ultimate reference
to labour, money is in fact deprived of any value: it has,
therefore, no economic 'autonomy'. The illusion that money is
autonomous is at work where financial 'production' of wealth
tends to replace the actual production of goods and where
automatic production processes are gradually substituted for
labour. The factor that generates value – namely, living effort –
becomes less and less prominent in the production process,
a tendency that should ultimately lead to the impossibility of
market economy:

> When the relation of the production process to the
> labour process obeys a tendency, the tendency of capital
> to increase indefinitely, and finds itself determined by it,
> this relation is specific to capitalism. Yet, at this point it
> becomes contradictory. For if capitalism strives to bring back
> production to labour, because only the latter is a source of
> value, it also does the opposite. It is not labour, but surplus
> labour that founds valorization, it is surplus labour that must
> be increased. But since the work day is limited – here again
> it is life that imposes its regulations on economy – increasing
> the surplus labour amounts to reducing the necessary labour,
> continuously increasing the productivity, and thus perfecting

and developing the technical and instrumental production indefinitely. (64–65)

The analysis of capital that Henry undertakes in 'Productive Forces and Subjectivity' (1974) and, in a more detailed manner, in volume II of the French edition of *Marx* published two years later, confirms this thesis. In capitalism, economic circulation does not aim primarily at exchanging goods (G) against other goods (G') through the universal medium of exchange that is money (M). Rather it aims at an increase in capital itself. The cycle GMG' transforms into MGM' (with M' > M), while the exchange of use values has been replaced by the maximization of exchange values. But how is such maximization possible? Henry's account of Marx argues that it seems as if economic circulation would somehow 'magically' lead to an increase in capital – magically because such an increase appears at first incomprehensible. If one presupposes, as classical theory suggests, that the value of goods is produced through labour, how can M transform into M' through circulation only? In other words, from where does the surplus value (*Mehrwert*) arise? Following Marx, Henry stresses that the aporia of circulation and surplus value can be solved only if one takes into account the particular good that is the 'labour force' (*Arbeitskraft*). As the term 'force' already indicates, however, this kind of good cannot be separated from living praxis, that is, from subjectivity, since labour is an essential modality of subjective life. Behind the façade of circulation and beyond the illusion of money as autonomous, the surplus value is created through the process of production that amounts to the process of human labour. For Henry, this has important consequences:

> The surplus value that had to emerge within the process of trade in reality takes birth outside of it. It does not stem from the apparent objective world of economics where everything seems to take place. In order to return to the source of surplus value, one must leave this loud universe and 'descend to the hidden abode of production'[2] that is nothing other than subjective life itself, the life of each worker. (34)

From this it becomes clear that the foundation of the economic is not the abstract labour of economic calculation, but the immanent reality of subjective experience. Thus, the economic is founded on something that is, as such, non-economic or *meta*-economic. Concepts falling under what Henry calls *pure economy* (*l'économique pur*) tend to veil this meta-economic aspect, since economics as a science considers a system in which there is no room for praxis, hence no room for its own foundation (a foundation to which it is oblivious). In the context of his phenomenological reading of Marx, Henry qualifies such an enterprise as fictional and the recourse to living praxis as necessary in order to understand economic reality from a genealogical point of view. This applies also with regard to capital and its composition.

What is capital and how is surplus value possible? The latter question seems to have found an answer through the concept of labour force, but this reference also affects the analysis of capital as Marx's critique of Ricardo and Smith shows: Is the eidos of capital to be determined through the distinction between fixed and circulating capital or rather through that of constant and variable capital? For Henry, a purely economic approach cannot provide an answer here because both distinctions are equally possible from a formal point of view. In the context of Marx's *Capital*, however, it appears that distinguishing fixed and circulating capital cannot account for the creation of surplus value:

> The economy, understood in its very foundation, sends us back to life. All the economic analyses of Marx accomplish this decisive return, this ultimate reference. As a consequence, Marx substitutes the economic opposition of fixed and circulating capital with a more essential one, in his eyes, namely that of constant and variable capital. Constant capital designates that part of capital invested in raw materials and instruments of production. (35)

Variable capital, on the contrary, refers to an aspect of capital that makes its valorization possible: the labour force insofar as it has the capacity to produce a value superior to the one required for its conservation and acquisition. It is the figure of '*life that brings on more than is given to it*' (36).

Henry's conclusion is, again, that a purely economic conceptualization leads us astray and becomes irrational when it does not acknowledge its necessary reference to immanent life. Even the very concept of variable capital still suggests that a certain value could increase on its own. But a value can have no effect at all without the intervention of the labour force. When

Marx distinguishes between fixed and variable capital, this distinction is therefore not founded on merely technical grounds but on philosophical ones, since he thereby distinguishes between the living and the 'non-living'. The latter is, for Henry, simply a figure of death, as the title of his 1984 article 'Life, Death: Marx and Marxism' suggests with its more than critical allusion to Marxism.

If, then, only the labour force can account for the creation as well as for the conservation of value, capital must be reducible to it. Formally, this means that constant capital (c) becomes $c = 0$, since it has no impact on surplus value: 'The opposition between constant and variable capital is essential because it is not an economic opposition. Its signification is ontological. Constant capital points to the objective element of the material process of production. Variable capital represents the subjective element of this process' (35). However, a continuous decline in the amount of labour force involved in the process of production has important consequences, as Marx's law of the tendential decline in the rate of profit illustrates with regard to the possibility of a market economy. The development of productive forces, in which objective factors become more and more prominent, leads to an increase in constant capital and, thereby, to a paradoxical decrease of the actual source of economic profit. Thus, a tendential decline in the rate of profit corresponds to a tendential augmentation of constant capital. Such is, for Marx as well as for Henry, the contradiction inherent to capitalism as it leads to a more and more automatized production process:

Activity is no longer a fact of the individual, a modality of a vital praxis and its actualization. On the contrary, paradoxically, activity becomes that of the machine, an objective process . . . it is the essence of the production that has changed: no longer defined by the subjective praxis, the production process has ceased to be a labour process, and here, the contradiction of capitalism explodes. (66; emphasis in original)

Surplus value, though at first glance incomprehensible, becomes intelligible through labour's ability to produce more than its conservation requires. The apparent ability of capital to increase itself is, in turn, explained through the role taken by labour in the production process. But, as this role continuously decreases, the systemic contradiction becomes manifest. From the beginning, both financial capital and industrial capital necessarily require labour in order to increase. Behind the façade of objective processes that seem to create value by themselves – for example, interest rates for financial capital, automatized production for industrial capital – it is the living subject as well as its effort or 'force' that are required for valorization to take place. This is why Marx considers profits gained by financial capital to be the effect of its role in the circulation process, while still not intervening in the actual process of production. This represents, therefore, the purest form of economic abstraction: 'This self-development of the economic as such is what Marx denounces. In this way, the economic is not only evil, alienation and an abstraction, it is also an illusion' (32).

If, however, the contradiction inherent to capitalist market economy leads to the gradual disappearance of subjective praxis in production, such an economy becomes, in turn, impossible. This enables the transition to *socialism*, a system characterized by the quasi-absence of subjectivity in the production process. As Chapter 3, 'Subjective Forces and Productivity', highlights, 'Socialist can only be said about (1) a society of overabundance, (2) in which the living praxis is no longer busy with production. The connection which unites these two fundamental meanings of the concept of socialism is, by the way, evident if the "surplus" does not mean anything else, eventually, than the "freedom" of the praxis' (88–89). Socialism is, according to Marx, a state in which subjective praxis is reoriented from the process of production towards the free development of individual faculties in education, art, science and so on, and which is tantamount to the end of alienation:

> Then the absolutely new historical situation is realized – will be realized – in which the life of men will no longer be confused, as it has been for millennia, with their 'material' life, that is, with the production of the necessary goods for their needs. Then will be born their new need, the need of their own activity as such and as living activity, as the *activity of their life*. (87; emphasis in original)

A critical point in Henry's interpretation of Marx concerns the original nature of praxis. From the point of view of the phenomenology of life, *social* praxis is reduced to individual praxis, the former being only the result of the intertwining of the latter and its representation in the context of society. Action is necessarily the action of individuals, never that of society as a whole or even that of a group. Society has no autonomous existence apart or independent from that of the individuals composing it. The primacy of individual praxis is, according to Henry, to be found in Marx himself, especially when Marx opposes Hegelian universalism in his 1842 manuscripts. In these writings Henry finds a reversal of Hegelianism insofar as Marx substitutes a genealogy of the concept of universality for its affirmation, putting real difference or heterogeneity before their determination through the whole. In this reversal of the part–whole relation, it is individuals who constitute society, not vice versa. Such a thesis is nonetheless problematic, especially considering the arguments of social determinism which highlight the extent to which individual choices are dependent on social background, society's class structure and so on in accordance, it seems, with Marx's concept of socio-economic classes. If, as Henry states, it is the individual that ultimately constitutes the reality of society, the totality represented by society and its history must be reducible to individual praxis. Moreover, this 'reduction of totalities' (society, history, even classes) is seen here as a specific Marxian achievement, despite the presence of Hegelian themes in the early Marx:

> If one retains only these Hegelian themes from the early writings, one persists in the classical Marxism of social forms, one finds confirmation there, but one forgets the 'no' of Marx to Hegel – the philosophy of Marx, the genealogy of these

forms, their reduction to a founding element that eventually is nothing else but concrete subjectivity – not the universal or the collective, but the individual . . . This reduction is the essence of Marx's thought . . . it leads us back to monadic existence. (16)

To be sure, determinations that characterize a totality such as a class are to be found 'in' the individuals constituting this class. The question is, however, whether these determinations can be thought of as 'autonomous', that is, as determining the individual 'from the outside' and independently of subjective praxis. Clearly, one does not chose one's social background and, thus, one's belonging to a certain social class. Specific and far-reaching conditions of existence are thus imposed on the individual, along with the representations they carry. For instance, Bourdieu's *Distinction* shows that even aesthetic preferences, which we usually deem to be highly personal judgments, are statistically correlated to social class belonging and seem to be determined by it. From this point of view, it is the individual considered apart from society, class and history that appears to be fictitious, whereas the determining and impersonal *structures* appear as the ultimate constituents of reality. As Marx writes concerning the capitalist in the preface of his *Capital*, 'Here, *persons* are dealt with only in so far as they are *the personifications of economic categories and are supportive of particular class-interests and class-relations.*'[3]

All of this might be granted, but even so it is necessary for a social determination to become an individual one, that is, to be integrated in the sphere of immanence. Without their actualization in subjective praxis, social determinations would remain purely external to individual life and, therefore, *un*real.

The 'autonomy' of social determinations is thus a paradoxical one. If such determinations seem, on the one hand, to be independent from the individual who is subjected to them, they nonetheless become real only insofar as they are individually experienced. If this is the case, however, then one will inevitably ask about the distinction that has to be made – within the scope of such individual life itself – between determinations that are social and others that are not. According to Henry, Marx has explicitly established such a distinction insofar as he identified labour (or, in general, the activity destined to satisfy material needs) as a part of subjective life. At its core, need is independent of social determinations. It originates in life as ipseity and as a self-generated movement with regard to which social determinations can appear, precisely, as constraints.

A second argument – again, taken from Henry's interpretation of Marx – is based on the idea that social relations (*rapports sociaux*) are engendered through and ultimately identical to individual praxis. The problem at stake here is one of reciprocal or circular causation. Social conditions seem to be produced by individuals who are, at the same time, subjected to them. They result from social activity, which *in fine* can only be situated in individual life (i.e. in the lives of a manifold of individuals). But, reciprocally, individual life is *conditioned by* the social world. As Marx already notes in *German Ideology*, 'circumstances (*Umstände*) make men as much as men make circumstances'. For phenomenological reasons, Henry rejects the idea of an external causation. In other words, there is no social causation that would not be reducible to individual praxis:

> The critique of the concept of society in Marx leads back to social classes. However, opposite to the direction in which Marxism went, classes do not constitute the ultimate principles of explanation but are realities that need to be explained. And what explains them is precisely the concrete life of individuals, their praxis, in such a way that it is the properties of the individuals, their habits, which form and determine those of their class. (45)

This model allows the integration of social determinations and immanence. It also accounts for the intergenerational transmission of social conditions: the inheritance of such conditions does not refer to some transcendent exteriority but to a *repetition* enacted by each individual through which social conditions are reproduced. Henry's model also speaks to the question of subjectivity's *mediations*, that is, precisely the conditions in which a subject's action takes place. As we have already seen, it is more than problematic to locate such conditions in a realm that would be completely exterior to the subject since, taken as purely objective, one does not see how they could become subjective and result in actual action. In addition to this, according to Henry's concept of reality outlaid in his 1963 *Essence of Manifestation*, the onto-phenomenological status of purely objective determinations would be that of unreality. A radically subjective approach such as Henry's, on the contrary, ensures the effective (and affective) reality of social conditions, although then it is difficult to see how they can be precisely *conditions*, that is, elements constituting a 'frame' imposed on individual life and action. Furthermore, to say that these conditions must be or *become* subjective in order to be effective does not a priori preclude a non-individual status for them. In fact, the very idea that the individual has to *reproduce* social conditions if they are to be effective tends to situate their origin 'outside' of individual subjectivity. This in turn conforms to Henry's analysis of alienation in *Marx*: the worker experiences the constraints of the workplace as alien to the development of his own subjective potentialities, and this experience is only possible insofar as there is a difference between these constraints (as *accidental determinations*) and the movement of subjectivity (as *essential determination*). The difficulty in accounting for social conditions both from a Marxian and a phenomenological point of view is explicitly considered by Henry in his debate with Paul Ricœur ('Rationality According to Marx', 1979), and also in his discussion of class (in 'Introduction to Marx') and ideology (in 'Life, Death: Marx and Marxism'):

[Marx] proposes a theory of the genealogy of the classes, of their foundation in the ontological realm. As such, the individual life discovers itself as the locus of this foundation. It is the determination of this life, the determination of individuals, their action and their thought that makes . . . that *is* the determination of the class. Marx says: 'The conditions of existence of the isolated bourgeois became the conditions common to all of them'. And still, in *The German Ideology*, some hundreds of pages further, he writes with absolute clarity: 'In the bourgeois class, as in every other, the personal conditions have simply become the common and universal conditions'.[4] (6)

It is the activity of each individual that immediately motivates his way of understanding the world and of thinking about himself. This arises in his own life without the mediation of any ideological, transcendent structure. It is because multiple individuals do the same thing and live in the same way that they also think in a similar fashion and that all these similar thoughts form, *after the fact*, what one can call the ideology of a class. (emphasis in original, 48)

Henry's account of social determinations, and the problem it raises, can therefore be summarized in terms of a conflict between essential and accidental determinations. The former are radically inherent to subjectivity; the latter are social mediations that are reproduced subjectively – for instance, through the division of labour. The factory constitutes a frame that conditions individual activity. From the standpoint of radical phenomenology, frames such as the workshop, the factory or the gigantic machinery of modern industry are nothing objective. Without them being experienced by someone, they would have no phenomenological existence: they would be nothing. But being experienced, they nonetheless appear in their differences, that is, in their respective impacts on subjectivity. If, therefore, mediations are dependent on subjective action in order to exist, it still makes sense to consider the ways in which some of them are alienating and others are not. The social world is always a world *to* the individual who experiences it, and the power to act is, for Henry, always rooted in individual subjectivity – nowhere else. As a consequence, Henry's account, and critique, of the concept of social praxis in 'Productive Forces and Subjectivity' is, to a certain extent, also a critique of Marx (see, for instance, 70).

If, for Henry, praxis is essentially individual, then social praxis can only describe the intertwining of individual actions. It is, however, clear that the result of such intertwining cannot be attributed to an individual. One can certainly object (with Henry) that this amounts to taking a general point of view, a mere representation without connection to the reality of the worker's experience and labour, for instance. But this objection appears to be no longer justified as soon as one considers the result of combined individual efforts as mediation or 'frame'. If we consider urban development as an example, it is obvious that 'no one' built the city as it is, since its development is a collective achievement, the result of a particular form of social praxis. From an Henryan point of view, this result is ultimately reducible to individual efforts, their combination and sum. And, seen from the 'outside', 'the' city remains a mere representation. But it is equally true that the city constitutes a frame or context where living activity takes place. Thus, the city, or at least part of it, is experienced individually to varying degrees. Urban development, as the result of social praxis, affects individual praxis far beyond the level of mere representation, and so do mediations or social conditions in general, as Henry's reflection on art and aesthetics (e.g. in *Kandinsky* (1988) but also in *Barbarism*) confirm. Put paradoxically, one could claim that mediations become real only insofar as they are experienced in the immediacy of subjective life. This, however, supports rather than contradicts Henry's claim that production as well as 'consumption' refer to *individual* praxis and experience. Thus, the concept of social praxis is the result of an abstraction that is, as an abstraction comparable to those operating in market economy:

> What the immediate position of individual labour as social labour means must be made clear. Either it means that the real praxis is inscribed in a collective production, but then one must recognize that this is always the case, in market economy as well as in socialist economy. Or it means the quantitative and qualitative norm whereby the praxis is subsumed for its definition and thus its retribution, the substitution of individual labour by general social labour, and then one must recognize that this substitution exists both in socialist economy and in market economy. (82–83)

This is why Henry's phenomenological reading of Marx is not only opposed to Marxist *theory* but also to the political regimes that came out of Marxism. It is in this sense that Henry even, and somewhat surprisingly, *opposes* socialism to 'communism' or 'communitarian socialism'. The latter, by removing the originally individual character of praxis and immerging it into the social, reproduces the process of abstraction that leads to alienation. If communist regimes try to 'reject the alienation constitutive of capitalism, the exploitation of man in surplus labour, [they do] not abolish the fundamental alienation of the market economy, the becoming different of the real praxis in "social labour". Indeed, it is this latter alienation that is targeted by socialism that Marx wanted to eliminate' (86). Socialism, according to Marx, thus aims at the end of alienation, that is, at the free development of individualities. But from the standpoint of the phenomenology of life, and although it incorporates this interpretation by means of Marx, such liberation requires overcoming an even deeper alienation – that of the 'forgetting of life' (*oubli de la vie*). The free development of individual life hence requires a rediscovery of subjectivity as life's absolute. Not subjectivity as turned outside towards the world, but as what affects itself and what is therefore the only power through which something can appear and become real, the only power through which there is a world. As Henry will emphasize in his trilogy on a philosophy of Christianity (*I Am the Truth*, *Incarnation* and *Words of Christ*), such liberation requires a rediscovery of absolute Life as Subjectivity – that is, a rediscovery of God.

Frédéric Seyler

Translator's Note

This collection of lectures by Michel Henry, in which he unfolds his unique interpretation of Karl Marx's philosophy, composes a fine introduction to Henry's two-volume work on Marx, which has only been partially translated into English.[1] Next to that, it also forms an introduction to Henry's thought as a whole, through the lens of Marx. The format of a spoken lecture urged Henry to repeat his point several times, in different wordings. However, in a written version too, these repetitions are highly appreciable: Henry's insight into Marx's thought, namely, that Marx was first and foremost a philosopher of subjective life more than he was a materialist, let alone a dialectical one, is not common at all. Henry wanted to argue against the abstractions of Marxism by returning to 'the sources', and thus to bring back Marx's thought to its essence, namely, a philosophy of life, as opposed to Marxism leading to death – an insight which he will also build upon in *From Communism to Capitalism*, for example, where he analyses both communism and capitalism as 'systems of death'.

My hope is that this translation will make Michel Henry's interpretation of Marx (and his work in general) accessible to the English-speaking reader. The introductory character of the texts gathered here also allows the reader to grasp concepts that Henry struggled with in his whole oeuvre: subjectivity, life, praxis. Together with *From Communism to Capitalism: Theory of a Catastrophe*[2] and *Barbarism*[3], this volume, *Marx: An Introduction*, is aimed at a larger audience and introduces Henry's metaphysical as well as political concerns outstandingly.

Although all three chapters have been translated into English in the past (and were separately published in journals in 1971, 1984 and 1974 respectively), my hope is that translating them afresh and bringing them together in one volume will increase their readability for the contemporary reader and once again show the unique value of Henry's Marx interpretation. I have translated the text from the original French. Compared to the already published translations, this translation might be regarded as a less literal one. However, it was my aim to stay close to Henry's 'spirit' in the sense that clarity of expression is one of Henry's main goals. His French is thus, almost in an un-French manner, very simple and precise. It is the very long sentence constructions that make the text sometimes difficult.

With regard to style, Henry uses many superpositions, associatively piled upon each other, which might sometimes make for a heavier sentence. As those constructions belong to Henry's personal style, I have chosen to keep them in English. It demonstrates Henry's writing process, his attempt to describe a controversial interpretation in a very precise way, and, while speaking and writing, correcting himself, redescribing his concepts continuously. I did shorten sentences that were very long (by cutting them in half, for example), in order to increase the accessibility of the text.

Finally, Henry uses both 'we' and 'I' to refer to himself and his intentions with the text. I have kept these references. Also, and presumably more problematic in our context, he always refers to human beings and individuals as 'men', 'he' and 'his'. Being convinced that Michel Henry meant this to be inclusive language, I have retained the male references. Replacing them with inclusive language would have made the text much heavier. Moreover, male references are also used by the frequently cited Marx himself, so that keeping them is more into accordance with the flow of the text as a whole.

For the translation of the citations of Marx, I have used the editions listed below (unless otherwise indicated) and abbreviated them in the endnotes. Where necessary to respect Henry's argument with regard to Marx's texts, I have modified the translation.

Karl Marx, *Grundrisse: Foundations of the Critique of Political Economy (Rough Draft)*, translated with a foreword by Martin Nicolaus, Harmondsworth: Penguin Books, 1973.

Karl Marx and Frederick Engels, *Collected Works*, London: Lawrence & Wishart, 1996; *Volume 4: The Holy Family*; *Volume 5: The German Ideology*; *Volume 35: Capital, Vol. I*; *Volume 36: Capital, Vol. II*. Karl Marx, *Surveys from Exile*, New York: Vintage Books, 1974 (including *The Eighteenth Brumaire of Louis Bonaparte*).

Karl Marx, *A Contribution to the Critique of Political Economy*, translated by S. W. Ryazanskaya, edited by Maurice Dobbs, New York: International Publishers, 1970.

I wish to thank my colleagues Samuel Pomeroy and Joseph Grabau, whose experience with translations and advice on the English language proved invaluable.

Dr Kristien Justaert, Leuven, 2018

1

Introduction to the thought of Marx

I

No thinker has had more influence than Marx, yet none has been more misunderstood. Marx is an unknown philosopher.[1] The reasons for which the *philosophical* thought of Marx has remained hidden until now, in at least partial darkness, are multiple. I will only mention here the principal reason: Marxism. Marxism puts a veil between Marx and ourselves. To be sure, Marxism definitely came forth from Marx. But it has followed its own path. Essentially oriented towards political action and its problems, it has only taken from the work of Marx what could be useful for its action, what could help it, clarify it for an evolving context. Certainly the theory was not totally neglected, because it becomes a force as soon as it penetrates the masses, but it is precisely this theory, a more or less succinct resume in service of the revolutionary praxis, that has been retained. Independent from this simplification, which was inevitable at this level,

Marxism has been more or less concerned with aligning itself to the scientific evolution; it has received a new illumination from it. However, even if this elaboration continued, certain fundamental philosophical texts remained unknown and unpublished. Their publication, coming after the constitution of Marxism–Leninism into a completed doctrine, didn't fail to provoke a certain surprise. This allowed us to measure the importance of the successive sedimentations that have come to cover up the original intuitions of Marx but mostly managed to distort them. It is a return to these original intuitions that we want to undertake. Such return presupposes the bracketing off of the specific content of Marxism, regardless of its intrinsic value. *The introduction to the thought of Marx is the ascent towards the origin of Marxism.*

We will first indicate how necessary it is to accomplish this return. For a long time, Marxism has been presented and is still being presented as a dialectical and historical materialism. But above all, Marx's thought does not have any deep connection to materialism. If one were to make an electronic inventory of the collection of Marx's texts – I mean those written by Marx himself – in which the term 'matter' or the adjective 'material' (which Marx uses more frequently) appear, we discover a certain number of significations, rigorously determined by their context, which eventually all point to one fundamental and decisive meaning. This ultimate meaning, the only one that can deliver the ultimate significance of Marx's philosophy, of what one calls his 'materialism', is 'subjective'. I will come back to this.

Dialectics plays only a secondary role in Marx. It is a Hegelian remnant that disappears progressively as Marx's thought distances itself definitively from that of Hegel. For Marx, there is no *dialectical essence*, understood as a force that runs through everything else, constituting its own internal law and ultimate reality, pure opposition, auto-movement of reality, founding this reality in its own negativity. The foundation of things, for Marx, is neither a unique movement, nor a universal force nor a process. When Marx talks about opposition or contradiction, he refers to something completely different. For Marx, the contradiction, the opposition, is never first. On the contrary, the terms of the contradiction themselves are never general entities, classes or structures, but particular realities, determined, singular. Particular realities are primary and everything that happens in the experience, the ins and outs and the conflicts that are produced, the more or less durable equilibriums that are installed, are nothing but the effect of these realities and their own determinations, their point of encounter.

What we just said about dialectics also applies to history. Let us consider, for example, a Marxist proposition: 'The history of every society up to our days, is the history of class struggle.' I say that this proposition, considered in all its force, does not make any sense in the eyes of the philosopher Marx. In order for such a proposition to make sense, one must first acknowledge that something like history exists. For Hegel, there is a history, namely, a reality that is substantially one, ontologically existent, and nothing else than the objectification of Spirit (*Geist*), which in turn is the unique principle of all reality. History is precisely the reality of this Spirit. Its concrete becoming is its phenomenal becoming and manifestation. History belongs to the phenomenology of the Spirit. And precisely because this phenomenal becoming is understood as finding its principle in pure opposition and negativity, history too is, by its own nature, dialectical.

Yet for Marx, this kind of history does not exist. History is not the self-accomplishment of a homogenous substance. It is not the realization of a universal and absolute reality. History, on the contrary, comes with presuppositions.

The German Ideology distinguishes three presuppositions that can be brought back to the explanation of the first. Marx writes, 'The first premise of all human history is, of course, the existence of living human individuals.'[2] The existence of these individuals implies, at every moment, that they satisfy the immediate needs of life, and therefore work, and that they transform their surrounding nature and thereby produce the necessities for life. This existence also implies that they reproduce themselves within the family, but in such a way that the needs of the family, their production, and work, can never be considered themselves as ultimate realities. Through them one can comprehend the particular individual who effectively responds to those needs, who accomplishes himself, in and through his body, this work and thus this production, and who maintains relationships with those who surround him – for example, with his wife – a relationship that is nothing but this relationship every time, this determined relationship, lived by him as a determined individual. Since *The Holy Family*, Marx rejects the myth of history, its absolutization. To Bruno Bauer who, like Hegel, subordinates man to the existence of a history of which he is only the mediation and who understands this history as the locus of truth, Marx opposes the radical objection of a philosophy of the individual: 'That is why history, like truth, becomes a person apart, a metaphysical subject of which the real human individuals are merely the bearers.'[3] And more: '*History* does *nothing* . . . "history" is not, as it were, a person apart, using man as a means to achieve *its own* aims; history is *nothing but* the activity of man pursuing his aims.'[4] There is no history, there are only historical individuals.

As he rejects the concept of history, for the same reasons, Marx rejects the concept of social class in the typical sense, namely, as a reality that has consistence and being in itself, dominates and determines the individual so that each individual can only be what he is, with his own characteristics, insofar as he belongs to a certain class, in and through his very membership. The class would in a way constitute the substance of its members. There would be, on the ontological level, a preexistence of class over the individual. In the margins of the manuscript of *The German Ideology*, Marx wrote, 'Preexistence of class for philosophers,' that is, for Max Stirner and the neo-Hegelians, the idealist philosophy that in Germany extends that of Hegel. And, indeed, the concept of class is a Hegelian concept, while for Marx the affirmation of the primacy of class over individual belongs to ideology. Let us read the text that copes with the note in the margins we have quoted. Marx writes, 'The statement which frequently occurs with Saint Max [that is, Stirner] that each is all that he is through the State is fundamentally the same as the statement that bourgeois is only a specimen of the bourgeois species; a statement which presupposes that the class of bourgeois existed before the individuals constituting it.[5] The rest of the text, pretending to describe the formation of the bourgeois class, in the form of a historical genesis, in fact proposes a theory of the genealogy of the classes, of their foundation in the ontological realm. As such, the individual life discovers itself as the locus of this foundation. It is the determination of this life, the determination of individuals, their action and their thought that makes the determination of class, that *is* the determination of the class. Marx says, 'The conditions of existence of the isolated bourgeois became the conditions common to all of them.' And still, in *The German Ideology*, some hundreds of pages further, he writes with absolute clarity, 'In the bourgeois class, as in every other, the personal conditions have simply become the common and universal conditions.'[6]

One must admit that here is an entire mythology, the Hegelian–Marxist mythology, that crumbles. According to this mythology, the substantial resides only in the transcendent masses that are called the State, the people, classes, social relations, relations of production and so on. The individual has no being unless he participates in these masses and inserts himself in their structures. It is true that for Marx, these masses continuously tend to become autonomous in the face of the individual, but this independence is in the end no more than an appearance, an illusion that is unmasked by reflection. The substance of the relations in which the individual is taken up is nothing but his own substance; the relations in which he inscribes his individual life belong to himself – they are the relations and the determinations of this very life. I quote again from *The German Ideology*: 'The conditions under which individuals have intercourse with each other are conditions appertaining to their individuality, in no way external to them.' And Marx adds a few lines further, 'These are the conditions of their self-activity and are produced by this self-activity.'[7] Because social relations are interior to the individual and mean nothing other than certain modalities of his personal life, the idea of a determination of the individual by the 'social' immediately appears absurd. It presupposes the abstraction of the social, its hypostasis outside of the individual as a reality different from him and the subsequent instalment of an external relation of causality between this alleged social reality and the individual himself. In this way, all individual and concrete subjective determinations are detached from their original reality, projected in a mythical heaven where they display a new existence as abstractions and present themselves to us as 'objective conditions'. Thus emerge the masses which are transcendently cut off from society as well as from history, class, the State, production, consumption and so on – all the structures and all the superstructures starting their fantastic tour, determining themselves mutually according to the purely verbal link of the most empty formalism. The old external causality that is affably guised by new words does not play any role, but in these abstractions, the individuals do not even intervene anymore in these pure systems.

Marx, however, never ceased to argue against such abstractions. He jeers at Stirner who believes that the State is a power above human beings. In commenting on this Stirnerian opposition between revolution or revolt on the one hand, and the existing state of affairs on the other, he writes, 'The whole senselessness of the antithesis that Stirner puts forward is evident at once from the fact that he speaks of "the Revolution" as a juridical person, which has to fight against "*what exists*", another juridical person.'[8] Who is this person whom you call all? Stirner asked, and he answered, It is society. And Marx comments, 'With the aid of a few quotation marks Sancho here transforms "all" into a person, society as a person, as a subject.'[9] Still criticizing Stirner, Marx starts to talk about the communist proletarians who upset society and who, he says, 'put the relations of production and the form of intercourse on a new basis – i.e., on themselves as new people, on their new mode of life.'[10] Talking elsewhere about social relations, Marx says that they are 'apparently independent of the individuals.'[11] What we call ideological formations must themselves be brought back to their ultimate origin. Talking about the first law that has ruled among men, Marx writes, 'The history of right shows that in the earliest, most primitive epochs these individual, factual relations in their crudest form directly constituted right.'[12]

I would say that the proposition 'the history of all societies until our days, is the history of the class struggle' does not make any sense to Marx. One will not hesitate to point out to me that this proposition has been written by Marx himself. It starts the first part of *The Communist Manifesto*. Does Marx then contradict himself? Or did we misinterpret it? What we are in need of now, clearly, is a *general theory of Marx's texts*, a theory, naturally, that also serves as a theory of the fundamental concepts of Marx's thought. And the moment we approach this problem, we may not forget the diverse theories of this kind that have already been proposed. The most recent is that of Louis Althusser and his pupils, to which we will restrict our investigation here. These authors were concerned with unveiling a radical seizure within the works of Marx between his earlier works that would only have a historical interest and in which the thought of Marx would still be dependent upon the philosophies of Hegel and Feuerbach and, on the other hand, the works written after 1845, the so-called mature works. The earlier writings would obey the ideological concepts of man and individual. The philosophy of man, for Althusser, is the 'theoretical foundation' of the thought of the young Marx. 'For the young Marx, "Man" was not just a cry denouncing poverty and slavery. It was the theoretical principle of his world outlook and of his practical attitude. The "Essence of Man" (whether freedom, reason or community) was the basis both for a rigorous theory of history and for a consistent political practice.'[13] It is only thanks to a radical 'epistemological rupture' that these concepts of man and individual are eventually evacuated from Marx's thought in favour of entirely new concepts – I quote, 'The concepts of social formation, productive forces, relations of production, superstructure, ideologies, determination in the last instance by the economy, specific determination of the other levels, etc.'[14] Simultaneously with the concepts of man and the individual, the concept of alienation is also eliminated, because alienation is the alienation of the essence of man, so that the concept of alienation is a 'pre-Marxist' concept that no longer appears in the later work of Marx, as can be seen, for example, in *The Introduction* of 1857. In this way, the ideology of the early Marx finds itself substituted by a theory that is finally scientific, the theory that is, by the way, not different from that of Althusser himself.

Such an interpretation can hardly be taken seriously. First, in no way does one observe in Marx's work the sequence of concepts that Althusser talks about, first man and individual, then productive forces, relations of production and so on. On the contrary, these concepts are simultaneously present; they can be found in the earlier writings as well as in the later works. The remark of Althusser holds only for the concept of man, of the essence of man. Marx has indeed abandoned this concept, not after his earlier writings but in these very early writings. The entire fundamental philosophical problem of the early Marx is precisely this rejection of the essence of man, the essence of the species, the *Gattungswesen* (humankind). However, Marx's problematic rejecting of the philosophy of the essence of man does not entail a dismissal of the individual *qua* real individual. On the contrary, it leads to the individual. But, one will object, is there a difference between the concept of man and that of the individual? There is the difference that divides the philosophy of Hegel and Feuerbach on the one hand, and that of Marx on the other. For the concept of man, or rather the essence of man, the essence of the species, is only, as Georges Cottier has convincingly demonstrated,[15] the last avatar of the Hegelian Spirit. It is the transposition into a materialist anthropology of this very essence that has reigned in the idealist ontology of Hegel as it has reigned within the romantic philosophy from which he began – and this essence is the essence of the universal. To the question of this universal, whether it is the flow of life – of which Hegel says in his *Phenomenology of Spirit* that it is indifferent to the nature of the wheels it turns – or whether it is the Spirit and its realization in the State – that is to say, the political essence or whether it is finally the 'genus' of Feuerbach, Marx gives a 'no', at the same time rejecting vitalism, idealism and materialism. The universal, the whole, the 'genus' does not come first. It is rooted, and what grounds it is what radically opposes it: the most radical and most particular determination – the individual.

It is true that Marx was first a Hegelian and that he has been influenced at a certain moment by Feuerbach. For example, we see this in his critique of religion in the *Contribution to the Critique of Hegel's Philosophy of Right*, where Marx defends the thesis that religion is nothing but the alienation from human essence, the projection of this essence outside of itself as a representation. And it is certainly true that the concept of alienation appears here in relation to the concept of man's essence, and that the concept of alienation is *thus* an ideological concept. Indeed, it is that of Hegel, taken over by Feuerbach and Bauer. It is the concept according to which alienation consists of a representation, an act of thinking. But the whole problem of the early Marx consists precisely in exceeding this ideological concept of alienation and rejecting it. His thesis, repeatedly reaffirmed, not only against Hegel and

Feuerbach but also against Bruno Stauer and Stirner, is this: if alienation really consists of an act of thinking – for itself, for the consciousness of the self or for the human essence – of an act of representing its content outside of itself, then, to overcome this alienation, it suffices to represent things differently, to stop representing one's essence outside of one's self. It suffices to think differently, to modify one's consciousness, one's mental structures or to accomplish some sort of 'epistemological rupture'. This thesis on alienation is precisely an ideological one, one of a German ideology, of philosophy generally understood as an ideology, to which Marx responds, in effect: you might very well represent things differently for yourself and change your concepts, but this has no importance. Thought cannot do anything against reality, namely, the living individual in the first place, with its existing determinations, because this real, living, determined individual is completely different from the way in which he represents things and the way he represents himself, his 'consciousness'. And without a doubt there is a relation between these two levels of being, between an individual's representation on the one hand, and what he is on the other; but this relation obviously finds its principle in the real individual, in his concrete existence, in his manner of being, in his way of living, so that this relation between the living individual and what he thinks is not a determined relation in the third person, but a phenomenologically grounded relation. 'It is not consciousness that determines life, but life that determines consciousness.'[16] The 'materialism' of Marx only signifies this phenomenological foundation of ideology in the concrete life of the individual.

How can one say then, that the concept of ideology appears in Marx only after 1845, when it manifestly constitutes the central theme of all his early writings, and in particular *The German Ideology*, and when Marx almost never talks about it anymore after that, precisely because his critique is made? How can one say that the concept of alienation is itself an ideological concept and that one finds it no longer in his mature texts, in *The Introduction* of 1857, when it is constantly present in the manuscripts of 1858–1859 and in *Capital* itself, when Marx has only put aside the ideological concept of alienation so as to better identify real alienation not as a product of thought but of existence? Even if it is true that there is an ideological concept of the individual, this concept has explicitly been acknowledged, described and rejected by Marx in his early writings, in *The Holy Family* for example, or in *The German Ideology*, so that the critique of the ideological concept of the individual has itself no other goal but to guide us back to the real individual.

It is true that we need a general theory of Marx's texts. This is the one I propose. It is suitable to distinguish, very schematically of course, three groups of texts in Marx. First the early writings until 1845, second what I would call the historical–political texts such as the *Communist Manifesto*, *Class Struggle*, *The Eighteenth Brumaire*, *Civil War in France* and so on, and third the economic texts and in particular the great works such as the *Grundrisse* and *Capital*, which I would be more willing to call the economical–philosophical texts. The historical–political texts are precisely those that have given birth to Marxism. The concepts that play a fundamental role in these texts are the concepts already mentioned, such as the productive forces, relations of production, contradiction, classes, revolution, dialectics and so on. These are the fundamental concepts of Marxism. They are the founding concepts of history. In this respect, their meaning is that of an origin, of a constituting power. But the fundamental concepts of Marxism, the founding concepts of history, are not the fundamental concepts of Marx's thought. With respect to ultimate reality, what they mean is no longer an original *naturans*, but a *naturata*, a founded reality, engendered, produced. The same is true for class, social relations and productive forces. There is a genealogy of these concepts as there is of the reality they refer to, and the first philosophy of Marx, distinct from his philosophy of history, is the analysis of this genealogy, the radical elucidation of the ultimate reality in which these principles of history themselves are rooted.

Thus one perceives the ambiguity of Marxism. The concepts it uses are true in a certain sense: it is true to say that in the eyes of Marx, the historian or political thinker, history is the history of class struggle. But these concepts become false when the reality they designate is absolutized, when, in the ontological order, this reality, always a general reality, is taken for the substantial and true being. They are further falsified when one believes that class or production themselves constitute the tissue of reality, its very essence and the foundational element of all particular determinations, for example of individuals. On the contrary, this was the meaning of these concepts in Hegel.

So this evidence is unveiled for us: from Hegel to Marxism, the kinship is blinding. It is the same primacy of the universal, the general, the social, the political essence, I would even say of the group, of the collective praxis, the dialectics, the negation, the revolution, of the internal movement understood as a universal essence working within all things.

One day, after I heard Jean Hyppolite talking one last time on the Hegelian texts of Jena – these texts that sound so surprisingly modern, so surprisingly Marxist, in which the central role of work appears, in which is affirmed that what counts is not what men say or think but what they do (one finds these famous themes, the critique of intention, of moralism, of the good soul, etc., in the *Phenomenology of Spirit*) – I asked him, 'But eventually, according to you, what difference is there between Hegel, Marx or Marxism?' And he answered, 'Well, in the end, there is no difference.' Since a long time, by the way, the interpreters who wanted to renew Marxism tore it off from the superficiality of a scientism or a neo-positivism like the Stalinist dogmatism of structures and returned again to a philosophy of universal negativity or rather to its anthropologization within a theory of collective praxis, of social praxis.

Yet what has contributed to enable this conclusion and finally this identification between the fundamental concepts of Hegel and those of Marx, are not only the historical–political writings of Marx, which we just talked about, but also his early writings. Indeed, we mentioned that Marx was first a Hegelian. There certainly is a rupture in his oeuvre, a rupture that we have situated within the early writings themselves. It is the radical rupture between the themes, the concepts, the properly Hegelian presuppositions and their negation by Marx, no less radical, at the moment when he, precisely, becomes Marx. If one retains only these Hegelian themes from the early writings, one persists in the classical Marxism of social forms, one finds confirmation there, but one forgets the 'no' of Marx to Hegel – the philosophy of Marx, the genealogy of these forms, their reduction to a founding element that eventually is nothing else but concrete subjectivity – not the universal or the collective but the individual.

There is not enough space here to demonstrate that this reduction is the essence of Marx's thought, that it leads us back to monadic existence. I will try to do it briefly. Let us recapture the genealogy of class. According to Marx, the division of labour grounds this genealogy. It is the division of labour that undergirds the first great social division between city and countryside. The division of labour in the rural factory and in the big industry shapes and determines the physiognomy of the proletariat. All socio-economic structures rest on this division. It grounds private property, the contradiction between private and general interest; it enables exchange, that is, market economy and, as a consequence, capitalism itself. As for socialism, its ultimate and most explicit goal is nothing but the suppression of the division of labour. What exactly is this division of labour? Of what does this ultimate and decisive phenomenon consist? Let us consider the individual, I mean one individual. Let us consider him as a subjectivity, not the subjectivity of idealism that exhausts itself in thought – universal thought – in representation, in what Marx calls with the classical philosophers 'consciousness'. Let us consider on the contrary the individual as a concrete, particular subjectivity, containing as virtualities a multiplicity of activities and possible intentionalities.

Marx calls these subjective potentialities 'personal forces'. Life as such, always as an individual life, is the subjective unity of these forces, which are themselves subjective, which rightfully belong to him, define his original being and are wanted by him as his needs. To live is necessarily to develop these kinds of possibilities. In *Capital*, Marx speaks about 'the free-play of his bodily and mental activity'.[17] To let these forces play means to actualize them, to give them being, reality. The realization of individual possibilities in no way means, like in Hegel, their objectification, their becoming manifest in the form of the object, in what is there before each and every one in work. On the contrary, the first realization of subjective virtualities is itself subjective. It is the actualization of them in life itself, as one of its moments, as one of its effective phenomenological modalities, as something lived. It is always an act or a state: it is consumption, pleasure, as the realization of basic needs, it is the act of self-movement, living movement, living work, it is the subjective aesthetic development of all senses. That is why the universal development of the individual that is continuously envisaged by Marx, and repeatedly demanded by him, is 'the full flourishing of the human interior'.[18] In the division of labour, the actualization of the totality of the individual subjective potentialities realizes itself in such a way that only one of these potentialities is realized in any given individual. The realization of the other potentialities, the other forces of life, falls outside him. They are realized in different monad spheres. Marx says in *The German Ideology*, 'The division of labor implies the possibility, nay the fact, that intellectual and material activity, that enjoyment and labor, production and consumption, devolve on different individuals.'[19] Each individual, considered in himself, cannot actualize the multiple possibilities of a life that nonetheless is his own, that constitutes his very being. When this individual being only partially realizes itself, it is mutilated. Division of labour, Marx says in *Capital*, 'attacks the individual at the very roots of his life', and further, 'it mutilates the worker to the point of reducing him to a fragment of himself'.[20] The ethical meaning of the critique of the division of labour is secondary. Its primary meaning is ontological; it presupposes a philosophy of the monadic subject. If one affirms the primacy of the universal or of the whole, however one conceives of it, the critique of the division of labour makes no sense. Indeed, from the perspective of the organism or of the structure, every part or each element fulfils its function by playing its role in the economy of the whole. It is only when one poses the point, or the element, as absolute, and the individual as the whole of being, that everything outside of the individual at the same time means an attack on his proper being. This outside is nothing other than that of which he is deprived. The critique of the division of labour is the theory of real alienation. The alienation is not ideological, nor is it political, social or economic, but rather it defines the interior state of the absolute monad. The division of labour is the division of subjectivity.

In addition to the early works and the historical–political texts, there is a third group of texts in Marx's *oeuvre*, the great economic writings of his mature phase. I would like to show in the next section, exclusively drawing on these texts, that the economic analysis of Marx is intelligible or even possible only if it is grounded in a radical philosophy of individual subjectivity.

II

One of the classical themes of Marxism is that apparent reality, recognized within human societies as that which supports and determines it, is an economic reality. Marx's thesis is that economics is only an abstraction. Economic reality is not the true, ultimate reality, but presupposes this reality and refers to it. This fundamental reality that grounds economics and ultimately determines it, is the individual subjective life. The whole economic problematic of Marx reveals itself to us as an analysis that traverses the economical as such, in order to arrive at its source, at its true substance, its real constituting sources. And it seems that these real determinants of economics are not themselves of the economic order but must be conceived of, on the contrary, as non-economical, or as an extra-economic reality, to use the expression of Marx himself. The solution to every economic difficulty, to each aporia of classical economy, consists precisely in the movement that we just indicated, in this return towards an origin, to a region of being that is heterogeneous to economics itself, even if it grounds it. So no more than it is the place of the reality, economics should not be the place of truth, or the place of the ultimate explication. On the contrary, the economical presents itself as an appearance, as an enigma and, eventually, as a mystification. And the analysis that comes to destroy this appearance, that solves the enigma, that clears away this mystification, is no longer an economic analysis, it is philosophy. It is clear then how wrong it is to present the evolution of Marx's thought as the progressive or brutal abandonment of philosophy after his early writings, then reduced to a simple ideology, and this to the profit of a positive and purely scientific study of the economy. The end of philosophy, always celebrated too hastily, doesn't mean more in the eyes of Marx than the end of Hegelian philosophy, and the theory of economy Marx proposes is indeed first of all philosophy since it rediscovers a meta-economic reality, precisely the reality to which the reflection of the early Marx was oriented. A prevailing unity in the thought of Marx thus runs through his whole oeuvre.

What, then, is the purely economic which Marx wants to reduce to a foundation outside of it? The analysis of economics as such is, for Marx, a true eidetic analysis, although it does not treat economics as such in general, but rather economics as it exists within a particular economic system, namely, market economy and, more precisely, market economy in its most advanced form: capitalism. The determination of the economic as such, the purely economic, is made by its dissociation from matter. And this presents itself to us from the beginning under its fundamental form as the individual, phenomenological life. It concerns life understood as basic needs and life which, through this fundamental experience of itself, transforms itself immediately in a corporeal motorial determination, in a living movement to fulfil these needs; in this way, all life becomes concrete activity destined to produce objects which conform to the basic needs, that is, conform to life itself, objects that are absorbed in this life through consumption or subsist outside life as a useful object. Such an object, produced by life for itself, is a 'use value': food, clothing, furniture and so on. The use value is a material object that nevertheless carries an essential axiological determination that expresses a decisive reference to life, to its precise usage, possible or real.

Yet let us immediately point at the ambiguity of the concept of use value in Marx, because use value does not only signify the objects useful for life. The activity that produces these objects is itself something that I can use and that I effectively use in the process just described. Every individual carries in himself a capacity to work, a 'labour power' that is his very existence, his body, his virtual motorial capacities. In other words, there is a use value of labour power that is simply the capacity of this power to actualize itself. But use value also has a third meaning: it does not only designate living labour, nor the product useful for life, but also the instrument that can be used during labour, the instrument or the materials that serve to life's functioning or maintenance. Oil, for example, can be consumed by man, but there is a special oil that can grease the machines. The use value of this oil is in the process of greasing.

However, considering the process that we have just described – the labour process – we need to make certain remarks. First, it seems that this process contains in itself or in its results nothing economical. The process focuses on work as a determination of existence, a moment of life and nothing else. When I am active, I accomplish all sorts of movements and *a priori* there is nothing economical in that; the instruments and the result of this work are, as we have seen, use values, and Marx says, 'Use value is not an economic form of value.'[21] Second, this labour process, material or real, is at once subjective and individual. Marx says in *Capital*, 'The elementary factors of the labor process are 1) the personal activity of man, i.e., work itself; 2) the subject of that work; and 3) its instruments.'[22] The texts in which Marx affirms that this personal labour is subjective are multiple; I cite randomly: 'subjective activity',[23] 'the subjective factor of labor power',[24] 'the pure force of living labor',[25] 'labor that is being done', 'labor in motion', 'labor in its subjective form', 'non-objectified labor', 'living labor', 'labor as a living subject'.[26]

That labour in itself is nothing economic but, on the contrary, an affirmation of individual life and probably its most essential realization can, for example, be seen in the critique Marx directed against Adam Smith's conception of labour as sacrifice. This is, as Marx teaches us, a purely negative conception that only counts for 'forced labour', that is, for labour within an economic system. But in itself, labour is not forced labour; it is a normal, spontaneous manifestation of life, a determination that belongs to life. Of course, work is not easy, it is not 'mere fun, mere amusement, as Fourier, with *grisette*-like naïveté, conceives it',[27] it is an effort and, what is more, 'the most intense effort', but as such, as effort, labor is existence itself, prior to any economic or historical determination. In Marx, there is an absolute theory of existence, what I would call a massive ontology, absolute ideas, transhistorical, irreducible to any ideology – in short, something like a pure philosophy. By way of example, let us cite this proposition: 'To the extent that it produces use value, that it is useful, labor is, independently of all forms of society, the indispensable condition of human existence, an eternal necessity.'[28]

The labour process, in itself individual, subjective, non-economical, constitutes the essence of the material process of production. This process, within Marxism understood as the material and economic basis of society and history, without a doubt plays a foundational role with regard to society and history, but it is in itself and first and foremost neither material nor economical. That the substance of the productive forces resides ultimately in the living subjectivity becomes evident when Marx declares, 'Men, developing their productive faculties, i.e., living.'[29] Because productive forces ontologically resolve into capacities, dispositions and activities of individuals, the development of these productive forces must signify the identical indefinite development of these individual activities. Marx says, 'The highest evolution of productive forces and thus . . . also the greatest development of individuals.'[30] Because capitalism brought about an unrestrained development of productive forces and, by that, of individual capacities, Marx sees in it the foundation of civilization.

Nevertheless, it is the concept of pure economics, of the economic as such, that we wish to define and, up until now, its elaboration has been negative, by way of exclusion from the economic everything that is material. What is left then? What are the characteristics of the purely economic? The objects produced to satisfy needs are not only use values, they are also exchange values. They become such when, instead of being consumed or used by their producer, an object is exchanged for another object. Such an object then becomes a commodity. The exchange value is a purely economic determination; it introduces us to the dimension of the economic as such. Pure economics is thus connected to exchange.

Historically, exchange was a marginal phenomenon; it appeared at the border of different groups of human beings when they were able to produce a little more than the immediate necessities for their survival. These groups have then exchanged the disposable products. Their production was barely affected by this exchange. Production remained essentially oriented towards use values, that is, towards consumption and life. Only surplus products became commodities, exchange values. Bit by bit, however, with the – albeit very slow – development of production, the exchange itself developed too, to the point that suddenly it has become the very goal of production. One did not produce anymore to satisfy one's needs, which, by the way, remained the same, and limited, so that production too remained limited. One now produced to sell, that is, one produced to produce and production became unlimited. The societies that reached this point in their evolution were turned upside down. A revolution had been produced, the only one, to be honest, in the history of humankind. This revolution consisted in the fact that production was no longer oriented or defined by use value, but by exchange value. It stopped obeying life to become, literally, economical production. Human activity, an essential mode of life, no longer founded its principle and goal in life itself, in basic needs; it stopped being the natural extension of life and the mode of its realization, and submitted itself to a strange teleology, a purely economic one, namely, the necessity to always produce more value, that is, more money. The activity submitted itself to the grand law of valorization. The substitution of use value with exchange value as the goal of production, that is, the arrival and reign of economics, signifies the perversion of everyday life and the reversal of all its values. For Marx, the economic is not the realm of reality, but rather the domain where reality is lost, the domain of its alienation. For Marx, the economic is first of all evil.

However, it does not suffice to describe first the intervention of exchange between groups of human beings, and then within these groups. At this point, we are not concerned with a historical genesis of market economy, followed by capitalism. It is the pure possibility, a priori, of exchange, that has to be revealed, and this possibility equals the possibility of exchange value or the economic as such. It is a matter of a transcendental genealogy of the pure economic.

To the question of the possibility of exchange value, classical economy responds: the origin of value is labour; the exchange value of a product is defined by the quantity of labour it entails. Marx, who first rejected this thesis, later quickly accepted it, because it was consistent with his secret concerns, namely, to demonstrate that the economic itself is rooted in life, that economic richness emerges from the labour of the workers.

But let us take a closer look at the process of exchange. Does classical economy really explain it? In the exchange, two use values, two products are put in each other's presence. They have absolutely nothing in common. On the one hand, it is a certain quantity of linen, on the other hand a certain quantity of wheat or metal or anything one would want. How can we establish an equality between all these products? One says, an equal amount of work was needed to produce these diverse quantities of different products, so they can be exchanged for one another. An equal amount of work was needed to produce x commodities m and y commodities m', so that x commodities m can be exchanged for y commodities m'. Only, there is this: for Marx, *the* labour doesn't exist. There are only concrete, individual, determined, subjective and qualitatively different labour processes. The qualitative differences of the use values presented on the market correspond to the qualitative differences of the individual labour that has produced them. How to compare weaving with spinning, with ploughing or with the work at the bottom of a mine? We need to give a radical meaning to this remark. For it is not only the diverse kinds of labour that are different. The 'same' work, done by two different individuals, is not the 'same'. If it concerns, for example, the unloading of a truck of coal and the carrying of the bags to a warehouse or a court, the effort of one worker, his subjectively lived activity, fundamentally differs from that of another worker. What may be painful for one could be lived by another as the positive application of his bodily powers and as the expression of his vitality. What bores one could be a matter of indifference to another. The time of their activity is not the same: their existences cannot be exchanged, they are not comparable and the real labour, its subjective temporality, a particular mode of a particular existence, is not exchangeable either. Marx knew all this. He wrote in the *Grundrisse*, 'Labor time itself exists as such only subjectively, only in the form of activity.' And a few lines further, he draws the conclusion: 'This statement means, subjectively expressed, nothing more than that the worker's particular labor time cannot be directly exchanged for every other particular labor time.'[31] But even if the original monadic life is irreducible to economy, exchange is necessary. At least, it happens in certain societies and thus it must be possible. One must construct the possibility of exchange from its own impossibility. Immediately after saying that particular, subjective labour cannot be exchanged for the individual that accomplishes it, Marx adds, 'Its general exchangeability has first to be mediated, it has first to *take on* an objective form, *a form different from itself*, in order to attain this general exchangeability.'[32] This different form, adapted by the real subjective labour in order to be able to be exchanged, is social labour. It is a certain quantity of social labour, a quantity that effectively defines the exchange value, which will be the exchange value of the product of this real labour. How is the transition made from real subjective labour to this quantity of labour that is made correspondent to it? How, in other words, is the genealogy of the economy derived from life? Through an abstraction. Economic, social labour, for Marx, is abstract labour. This abstraction takes on diverse forms. One substitutes the exterior frame of the effort of the living subjective labour with the temporal objective frame, measuring work by the day, the half-day, the hour. This activity becomes that many labour hours. For the quality of this activity, for its own subjective difficulty, one substitutes a prototype, the prototype of simple labour or complex (qualified) labour. One will estimate, for example, that one hour of qualified work equals two hours of simple labour. Eventually, concerning the necessary labour to make a random product, one will substitute, again, the actual labour of a random worker with the idea of the quantity of energy that he should normally use to obtain the result in question. The necessary labour is thus no longer the labour that is actually accomplished but the idea of the labour to be accomplished, an ideal norm of labour understood as an average and defined in an abstract way.

This distinction and this opposition between real and abstract labour is given by Marx as his own discovery and as essential, as worthy of a fundamental elucidation that we have just retraced. I quote *Capital*[33]: 'I was the first to point out and to examine critically this twofold nature of the labor contained in commodities. As this point is the pivot on which a clear comprehension of political economy turns, we must go more into detail.'

The distinction between real and abstract labour is indeed essential. First of all, it allows us to elucidate the nature of labour in its double relation to value and product, in its relation, if one prefers, to the commodity, as both an exchange value and a use value. Social labour grounds exchange value, real labour grounds use value. But this foundation accomplishes itself in a twofold manner. Exchange value is the objectification of social labour, as shown in this passage of the *Grundrisse*: 'The objectification of the general, social character of labour (and hence of the labour time contained in exchange value) is precisely what makes the product of labour time into exchange value; this is what gives the commodity the attributes of money.' A few lines further, Marx says that money is 'the objectification of general labor time.'[34] But if the relation of abstract social labour to exchange value can be described within the Hegelian scheme of objectification, we cannot do the same with the relation of real, living labour to the produced object. Living, real labour, cannot be objectified; it creates the product or rather transforms it. This transformation concerns the product, not the labour which is and remains subjective. Marx writes in a decisive manner: 'Labor time as subject corresponds as little to the general labor time which determines exchange values as the particular commodities and products correspond to it as object.'[35] The analysis of living work thus shows us how, on the level of ultimate reality, Marx challenges Hegelian ontology as well as any (form of) objectivism.

Second, the distinction between real and social or abstract labour elucidates definitively the enigmatic, 'phantom-like' character of value. As we just saw, exchange value is the objectification of social labour; as such, value has its own economic specificity and is irreducible to the material properties of the thing that has value. Marx continuously denounces the confusion between economic and material determinations, a confusion that he depicts as fetishism, economic materialism and so on. In commodity exchange, value appears to be a property of the products – that is precisely the fetishism of the commodity – while it is only the expression of a social reference, that of the labour objectified in these products. But the labour materialized in value is only defined socially, economically, abstractly, each time we talk about this many hours of social labour, of necessary labour. However, because social labour expresses the real labour of which it is the abstraction, value refers secretly to the real being of individual, living labour; that is its ultimate foundation. The status of the economic becomes decidedly clear: after having demonstrated the alienation in it, the reversal of the immanent teleology of life, Marx now determines its genealogy in a positive way; by assigning it a foundation in individual life, but through the mediation of social and general labour, he depicts the economic explicitly as an abstraction.

That the economic is an abstraction, the abstraction of concrete, subjective life, and that it necessarily leads back to it, that is what not only shows its very possibility, the possibility of value, but even more its development. This produces and culminates when value becomes precisely the end of production. Production is then no longer directed towards the satisfaction of needs, to use value but, on the contrary, aims at the creation and increase of value as such, when production simply puts value into value. This is what happens with capital: the material process of production becomes a process of valorization. The transformation of the material process of production in a process of valorization presupposes that all the material elements of the production process are convertible in value. Not only the result of the process, the product or use value must be capable of being exchanged; the raw material, the instruments of labour and the auxiliary materials, and the living labour itself, also have to do this, that is, propose themselves on the market as exchange value, as commodity.

Concerning living labour, that is to say, the worker, his appearance on the market under the form of an exchangeable commodity is connected to certain historical conditions that are the historical presuppositions of capitalism. For the worker to present himself on the market, he cannot have anything else to offer, he cannot have made any product himself, and he must be deprived of any instrument or means of production. Marx described the large social phenomena that have led to this result at length – essentially the rural exodus following the occupation of land by big landowners, the replacement of agriculture by stock breeding and so on. Such phenomena, however important, merely constitute the precursors of capitalism. We must dive into its intimate nature now.

The value of the different elements of the material process of production is fixed in accordance with the general law of value, that is, it is determined by the quantity of social labour needed to produce each of these elements. The raw material, the instrument of work, costs so many hours of labour; it has this much value. Concerning the labour power that the worker presents on the market, its value is that of the necessities to keep him alive. The quantity of the labour needed to produce these necessities, that is, for example, the maintenance of the worker during one day, is the value ascribed to the use of his labour force during this day.

If every element of the material process of production has a value, is exchangeable on the market and can be sold, it can also be bought. That is what the capitalist does. With a certain sum of money, he buys the various elements – raw material, instrument, labour hours – necessary for the production of a certain product. His aim is not the fabrication of a product but the selling of it and, with this sale, obtaining a bigger sum of money than what he has invested. From this whole process, he thus withdraws a greater value than what he had invested. This greater value is the surplus value. The second enigma of the economy, after the one of value, is of surplus value: Where does it come from?

The answer of Marx is that no economic determination is capable of producing surplus value, itself an economic determination. If one considers the capitalist process, that is, the economic process of production, this process, as we saw, reveals itself as a process of valorization, a process in which a certain value – the value invested by the capitalist – is transformed into a greater value, as if value, exchange value or economic value had the power to increase in value itself. This self-development of the economic as such is what Marx denounces. In this way, the economic is not only evil, alienation and an abstraction, it is also an illusion. To unmask this illusion, to lift the veil of the economy, is to rediscover the reality behind it, the concrete individual subjectivity.

First of all, it is clear that exchange value does not have the power to increase itself. When I exchange one commodity for another, the new commodity that I possess is materially different from the first one – I had wheat, now I have iron – but the value remains the same. Or I can exchange a commodity for money (a sale), or money for a commodity (a purchase), but in all these cases the value of the commodity equals the value of the money obtained or spent in the exchange. As a consequence, the endless process by which commodities are incessantly exchanged is such by nature that the exchange value cannot increase. On the contrary, this value, which is incarnated in constantly different products, and which undergoes metamorphoses into always diverse substances, always remains identical. Economic circulation cannot create surplus value. Yet outside of it, that is, outside of all the connections of the exchanging producers, there is nothing. Moreover, the surplus value or the capital that results from this 'cannot emerge from the circulation, but cannot not emerge from it; at the same time, it has to and has not to be born from it'.[36]

Let us first look at how surplus value emerges in the process of trade, that is, in an exchange, but in a very particular exchange, which comes between capital and labour or, more exactly, between a capitalist and a worker. This exchange consists of the following: the capitalist gives to the worker the exchange value of his labour and in return he receives from the worker the use value of his labour; this means that the capitalist gives to the worker a value defined by the quantity of work needed for the production of the necessities the worker requires during one day; in return, he receives the actualization of the worker's labour power during this day; or, to put it more simply, the capitalist gives to the worker the value corresponding to the maintenance of his life during the day, and in exchange he receives the activity of this life during this day or a part of this day. Is there an equivalence between the exchanged terms? No, because life has the absolute, even metaphysical, property to produce more than is necessary for its subsistence. On the one hand, during his labour day, the worker produces what is necessary for his maintenance or at least a value that is the equivalent of it. In this way he reproduces, that is, returns to the capitalist the exchange value that the latter pays him in the form of a salary. But on the other hand, the worker creates something more than is necessary for his maintenance and, at this level, he gives the capitalist a second value for which he doesn't receive any equivalent. This second value is surplus value. Marx writes, 'The only extra-economic fact in this is that the human being does not need his entire time for the production of the necessaries, that he has free time at his disposal above and beyond the labour time necessary for subsistence, and hence can also employ it for surplus labor.'[37] And we see that precisely this unique extra-economic fact determines the whole capitalist economy or, in fact, all possible economy.

With the introduction of this extra-economic fact, we now understand that the surplus value that had to emerge within the process of trade in reality takes birth outside of it. It does not stem from the apparent objective world of economics where everything seems to take place. In order to return to the source of surplus value, one must leave this loud universe and 'descend to the hidden abode of production'[38] that is nothing other than subjective life itself, the life of each worker, in his creative capacity, to exalt himself beyond his own conditions, to transcend them, to present something beyond these conditions, something that was not there before. The actualization of this creative capacity is the use of labour power – it is its use value. The worker offers this use value to the capitalist for an exchange value that is not only unequal to the use value but also heterogeneous to it. To say that the labourer presents the use value of his labour power is to say that he presents his life, as a force of growth, as a power of transcending his own conditions. It is because use value eventually points to living labour that it is the fundamental concept of economy. Marx says, 'Labor does not confront capital as a particular use value but as the use value in general.' Yet use value, the fundamental concept of the economy, is not itself an economic concept. Here again the economy, understood in its very foundation, sends us back to life.

All the economic analyses of Marx accomplish this decisive return, this ultimate reference. As a consequence, Marx substitutes the economic opposition of fixed and circulating capital with a more essential one, in his eyes, namely that of constant and variable capital. Constant capital designates that part of capital invested in raw materials and instruments of production. Variable capital designates the part of capital that serves to pay the salaries, that is exchanged for labour power. The opposition between constant and variable capital is essential because it is not an economic opposition. Its signification is ontological. Constant capital points to the objective element of the material process of production. Variable capital represents the subjective element of this process. To penetrate the secret of capital, it suffices to blot out everything that is objective within the process of production. It is not without surprise that, in the middle of all the calculations with which Marx overcharges *Capital*, the reader will find this equality: c, constant capital = 0. Of all the investments of the capitalist it suffices, eventually, to remember only the sum that he has dedicated to salaries. A certain industrial has given the workers 90 pound sterling; 90 pound sterling dedicated to salaries, but this sum is fixed. How can it then vary, increase, increase the capital? The sum given to the worker, to be clear, does not vary; it is well-fixed. But the capitalist has exchanged it for something that varies, that is the variation itself, that is the metaphysical power of all variation and of all growth: *life that brings on more than is given to it.* With the elimination of constant capital, and the elimination of the 90 pound sterling given to the worker, a last goodbye is given to the ciphers and to science. There is room for knowledge. Knowledge is always the knowledge of the most simple thing; it is the knowledge of life, of which the internal law is the law of the world and its development. But to arrive at this knowledge, one must perform a return to the origin, the *epoche* of science and of all ideological sediments – this *epoche* that might indicate to us the philosophical task that is ours today: to read Marx for the first time.

2

Life, death: Marx and Marxism

On the occasion of the hundredth anniversary of Marx's death,[1] has the moment not come to finally make a fair judgment, one possible only in hindsight, on the man that we do not know how to describe – philosopher, economist, historian, sociologist, politician, theoretician of the worker movement, reformer, revolutionary or prophet? And this judgment, finally putting everything in its place, could it not take the form of a response to the famous question: What is dead and what is still alive today of his oeuvre, equally monumental and diverse since it touches all domains of knowledge and action?

Only, unlike Hegel (whose speculative teaching Croce wanted to re-evaluate in the light of history), isn't what Marx brought for humanity, besides a theoretical corpus equally immense – in accordance with his most explicit intention: 'Philosophers have only interpreted the world in different fashions, what matters is to transform it' – something wholly different, an upheaval not only of thought but of the societies themselves, of the lives of hundreds of millions of individuals? While every superior and elaborate form of comprehension by man of his relation to the world, every religion, every mythology, every moral, every 'world view' only influences bit by bit, through the mediation of consciences, in the way of life, we find ourselves here in the presence of a totally exceptional phenomenon: the direct, decisive and brutal action of a philosophy upon reality in its most trivial and yet deepest sense on everyday reality. Do we not have to turn to the regimes and the peoples that have pretended to organize themselves and construct their fate in light of the conceptions formulated by Marx? Concrete results, a tangible historical situation, objectively analysable according to the multiple methods available to the human sciences, effective developments within the domains that essentially characterize a society – economic, social, cultural – all this, does not it constitute, in order to judge the thought and the oeuvre of Marx today, a more certain and incontestable guide than simple theoretical writings?

In no way. One must recall this determinant fact that is ever and again occult, that the thought of Marx has no connection to Marxism and that it is only Marxism that has served as a model and a lead principle for the construction of new societies that have wanted and believed themselves to express the socialism as conceived by Marx. The history of Marx's thought after his death, which became the history of Marxism, represents in fact the most exceptional and the most astonishing cultural phenomenon that can be perceived in modern times. True, every great doctrine, because of the inevitable game of influences and interferences, has undergone more or less profound modifications and alterations.

By way of example, consider the immersion of Christianity in Greek thought. It is the task of historians to unravel the threads tangled by these ideal, spiritual or moral sequences. In the case which concerns us here, something else is at stake: *the totality of the fundamental philosophical writings of Marx – in particular the* Critique of Hegel's Doctrine of the State, *The* Manuscripts of 44, The German Ideology – *remained unknown to those who constructed the Marxist ideology and built the world in light of this ideology.*

Which theoretical basis, properly philosophical, did they have – Lenin, Trotsky, Stalin, Mao and some others, including intellectuals such as Plekhanov? Of these above mentioned writings, which remained unpublished because they were uncompleted or explicitly refused by the editors (e.g. in the case of *The German Ideology*), Engels wrote, after Marx's death, a summary which had to serve as the foundation for the whole theoretical edifice of Marxism: he titled this summary *Ludwig Feuerbach and the End of the Classical German Philosophy.*

It is a text of extreme intellectual weakness that essentially puts before us the following alternatives: either the spirit created matter, as Hegel and all the idealists believed, or else the opposite – matter created spirit, its own reflection in the consciousness or in people's 'brains', as Marx said. This is what inaugurates the new philosophy (new!) and determines the way in which it is, since then, suitable to approach all great thought of the past, dissociating in each of them the idealist and bourgeois elements that it still contains, precursors of materialism and of the future.

It is a historically inexact text because, in the prodigious philosophical evolution of Marx in the course of the years 1840–1847, he inverted the decisive influences of Feuerbach and of Stirner, placing the latter before the former, whereas it was the reading of *The Ego and His Own* that guided Marx, who became fully aware of his deep thought, already formulated in the *Critique of Hegel's Doctrine of the State*, to break with Feuerbach and his philosophy of the *Gattungswesen*, one of the by-products of the Hegelian universe.

The text is philosophically incorrect because it speculatively places underneath every being a matter that is physical, and of which Marx never speaks. Marx uses the adjective 'material', by which he in effect means reality, not the objective reality that science analyses and of which it pursues the infinite elaboration, so that this reality still presents itself today as an X – adequate knowledge of which refers to the ideal term of scientific progress. By 'material' Marx understands the reality that we are, and of which we are ourselves the immediate proof, the *individual phenomenological life*, this undeniable need of which we feel the pressure and which spontaneously expresses itself in the activity that it develops in order to satisfy itself.

However, on the one hand it is this phenomenological life as it expresses itself, a sort of absolute, that constitutes the foundation of history and of economy in the sense that it produces the specific phenomena that will be studied by the sciences we call history and political economy. Life is not the object of these sciences; it produces the phenomena that will possibly be submitted to their investigations, the *naturans* of the formations that will be made objective by the scientific approach, but that in themselves, that is, in the life that produces them and does not stop producing them, are nothing of the kind. 'Historical materialism', if one wants to retain this term which does not come from Marx – *The German Ideology* rather speaks about the 'material foundation of history' – is not one particular conception of history among other possibilities, but a philosophy of history that assigns to 'historical' phenomena an origin situated outside of them, precisely in life, that as such appears as the metaphysical foundation, or in any case the meta-historical foundation of history itself. It is, within life, the indefinite repetition of needs and labour; it is the suffering and acting individuals, 'the living human individuals', Marx says, who are 'the first premise of all human history'[2] and who as such determine this history a priori, and every possible society as a history and a society that are and must necessarily be first of all a history and a society of needs and of labour, of production and of consumption.

On the other hand, this life that appears as the principle of history and of society is not, for Marx, the object of an external designation. It does not present itself as an empirical reality, as the theme of a science which is itself empirical. And here one must try to recognize the originality and the extraordinary penetration of Marx the philosopher. It is in a properly philosophical debate with the greatest philosophers and with Hegel, the one who incarnates all of them by recapitulating and assuming their thoughts in the *Aufhebung* of his system, that the proper contribution of Marx to Western philosophy is defined, namely, the interpretation of original being, of what constitutes the foundation of everything and particularly of history and society, as life. What is alive in Marx is, first of all, that he is a thinker of life.

A unique position, indeed, had to be conquered *against* classical philosophy, which was a philosophy of thought, interpreting man as a thinking being, as a reasoning or rational animal. But what was important in such a perspective was not that man, primarily identified with thought, posited himself at the same time as the Subject for whom all the rest was nothing but an object – *his* object – so that the reversal of the primacy of the Subject to the profit of the Object, was conceivable (as did Engels, in his way); it was, in a much more essential way, that the relation of man and being is a relation of exteriority, the Subject–Object relation, in whichever way that one eventually chose to read it, or whichever term that one privileged in it.

But if one considers more precisely the philosophical positions on which Marx reflected in the course of his prodigious theoretical work of the years 1840–1846, namely, the *thought* of Hegel and the *intuition* of Feuerbach, one sees that it is this relation to being as a relation of exteriority that defines both of them, and that it is precisely this relation that Marx will challenge brutally. For Hegel's dialectic only describes this process of objectification of which the last chapter of the third *Manuscript of 44* presents an admirable critique which, at the same time, prohibits that one searches for any reality in it. Whereas Feuerbach's intuition (materialism) inverts the subject–object relation in favour of the latter – because, unlike Hegelian thought, sensible intuition no longer creates its object but becomes receptive of it – at least it conserves, by defining being as that which one reaches through the senses, this decisive ontological determination of reality as external reality.

Yet the relation of life to itself is not a relation of exteriority. The one who desires, who is hungry, who carries a burden, who carves a stone, who uses his body through any of its powers, this person does not install between himself and his desire or his effort a distance through which he would be able to escape from what he does or what he is; but rather, immersed in himself and fundamentally passive in relation to his own being, he coincides with himself to be what he is, insurmountably. Life is a radical immanent dimension by virtue of which it expresses itself without ever being separated from itself, and it is as such, in continuously expressing itself, that it is life. This original dimension of being, as without any distance and any difference, as life, is what Marx calls 'praxis'.

If the *Theses on Feuerbach*, in which the concept of *praxis* emerges, is difficult to read, it is because (to say what has never been said), like every researcher put in this crucial situation where a decisive discovery is going to be made, Marx finds himself naturally deprived of appropriate conceptual means. To reject Hegel's dialectic, he only has at his disposal Feuerbach's materialism, just as he only has Hegel's dialectic available to reject Feuerbach's materialism. Materialism and dialectic represent, at the heart of their common essence, what must be radically and conjointly eliminated, so that the road towards the essential thought by Marx under the title of praxis is opened. To express this essence that is life, the fundamental concept of

Marxism that unites the two terms which Marx put out of play, namely, 'dialectical materialism', constitutes the quintessence of absurdity.

If one wishes to measure the gap or rather the abyss that separates the thought of Marx from Marxism, one must add that praxis in its essence is individual, and this because it is first of all a corporeal praxis, the development of an 'organic subjectivity' as the *Grundrisse* will formulate it, which is always that of an individual and can only be thought in connection to it. This concrete praxis, this organic subjectivity will become, in *Capital*, the 'living labour'. And here is why, to say it immediately, every economic analysis will take as criterion and as exclusive reference the labour of a worker: what is valid of the labour of an individual worker, according to *Capital*, is valid for the labour of a whole working class. It will construct itself from this singular labour which appears as the starting and endpoint of the entire economic system and as its unique *naturans*.

But above all, it is the sociological analysis that is intelligible only when starting from the living individual. The Marxist idea, confirmed by the theses of the school of Durkheim and recently recapitulated by structuralism, of the apparent and evident primacy of society over the individual, and the interpretation of the relation that unites society and the individual as similar to the relation in which a whole determines its parts (a thought already dear to Hegel) – all this had been turned into a mockery by Marx in his polemic against Proudhon. Because, indeed, Proudhon supported, before the fact, a Durkheimian thesis by affirming the specificity of the laws and the social phenomena irreducible to individual characteristics or rather preceding them and thereby determining them, like a cause. 'The life of this society,' Marx writes ironically, 'is guided by laws, the opposite of those which govern the activities of man as an individual.'[3] It is thus the laws of life within the individual, the laws that 'make him or her act', that determine the structure of a society. And thus all social activity, which apparently takes place outside of us, following seemingly objective rules, in reality finds its prefiguration and laws in ourselves and in our living subjectivity. Men always follow roads already walked. These are not roads we find outside ourselves or that other men have taken before us. The roads we follow are traced within us, the lines and the impulses of our body and these paths will not mislead us. They describe the circle of our possibilities and assign to our life its destiny, as well as the form to every society.

The critique of the concept of society in Marx leads back to social classes. However, opposite to the direction in which Marxism went, classes do not constitute the ultimate principles of explanation but are realities that need to be explained. And what explains them is precisely the concrete life of individuals, their praxis, in such a way that it is the properties of the individuals, their habits, which form and determine those of their class. 'In the bourgeois class, as in every other, it is only personal conditions that are developed into common and universal conditions.'[4] And, 'Personal relations necessarily and inevitably become class relations, and as such become fixed.'[5] It is thus a fallacy that consists in turning everything 'upside down' that pretends to deduce the reality of an individual from that of the class he or she belongs to, a fallacy first committed by Stirner before it was taken over by Marxism and violently denounced by Marx himself: 'The statement which frequently occurs with Saint Max that each is all that he is through the State is fundamentally the same as the statement that the bourgeois is only a specimen of the bourgeois species; a statement which presupposes that the class of bourgeois existed before the individuals constituting it.'[6]

That it is the concrete way of life of the individual that realizes the properties of a determined class and not the other way around, is what Marx has demonstrated in a decisive way with regard to one of these properties: ideology. For, every class has its ideology and what is more evident and natural than to explain, here again, what a given individual thinks starting from the 'ideas' of his own class or of his own era. However, it is true – and this is one of Marx's most fundamental theses – that for him, the world of ideas in the broadest sense is not autonomous and finds its foundation in life itself, because it is the representation of this life. This ensemble of ideas, of thoughts, of images, of representations of all sorts, this mental structure, this is what Marx calls consciousness. Consciousness, for Marx, does not mean the immediate proof that each person makes of his own life, his suffering, his needs, his efforts, but the way in which he represents life and spontaneously interprets it. And Marx's decisive intuition is precisely that the way in which men understand and interpret their own life is not free but depends on this life and is rooted in it. In this way, the following famous text can be explained: 'It is not the consciousness of men that determines their life, it is their life that determines their consciousness.'[7] It is their life, their own, personal, individual life, the concrete mode of their everyday activity – in no way the preexistent ideology of an objective class. For no objective reality, social class or Engels's matter has the power to produce an idea: only life can do this. What Marx affirms is precisely the determination of life by the deepest modalities within ourselves, which are the affectivity and the corporeal praxis of these representative, intellectual and spiritual modalities, of its 'consciousness'. He affirms the continuity which reunites, in an individual's subjectivity, the former (the idea) to the latter (life), making of them an ideology, according to his admirable formula: 'The language of real life'.

This is what the analysis of the French peasant class in the middle of the nineteenth century establishes in an incontestable way. In this respect, this analysis is crucial.[8] What characterizes the situation of these peasants is the dispersal of families over a great number of isolated parcels, the nonexistence among them of any relation other than a purely local one, the absence of any political, cultural or spiritual community, of any ideology in the sense of an ideal objective and intersubjective reality, of an ensemble of representations or of ideas, consigned to books, transmitted by education, announced by newspapers, having in whatever form an effective existence, capable as such to define the horizon from which would be explained the thought of all those who are subject to it. How then could an ideological horizon determine the thought of French peasants in the middle of the nineteenth century when this horizon did not exist?

And still, all these peasants think roughly the same thing. The similarity of their views was expressed, for example, on the political level by their support of Louis Bonaparte, thereby enabling his *coup d'état*. This similarity of thought and of 'ideological reflexes', and the absence of any objective determinant, can only be explained by its concrete subjective genealogy: it is the activity of each individual that immediately motivates his way of understanding the world and of thinking about himself. This arises in his own life without the mediation of any ideological, transcendent structure. It is because multiple individuals do the same thing and live in the same way that they also think in a similar fashion and that all these similar thoughts form, *after the fact*, what one can call the ideology of a class.[9]

This question of the status of the concept of class in Marx is very important from the political point of view. We know the role assigned to the proletariat in the struggle for the emancipation of man with regard to all forms of alienation that weigh on him, and the proletariat is a class. So there are two ways to consider 'class': as an a priori or as a totality existing by itself and for itself, an autonomous entity gifted with a life of its own and acting like it, struggling in the way a global power fights against another power of the same kind, another 'class' in fact – the bourgeoisie. History then takes the form of a gigantic confrontation between antagonistic forces; it is 'the history of class struggle'.[10] In its turn, this confrontation takes on a messianic scope because such is, in the texts prior to 1845, the meaning of the proletariat itself. As an autonomous reality, even if it is an alienated reality in the system of exploitation of labour, the proletariat has to push alienation to its limit and suffer it to the end so that, from this excess of misery and suffering, redemption emerges. As a class 'which, in a word, is the complete loss of man and hence can win itself only through the complete re-winning of man',[11] the proletariat inaugurates a drama that is only the secular transposition of a sacred history from which it borrows all its prestige: that of Christ himself.

Yet if the proletariat is, like every other class, nothing but the result and the effect of the concrete praxis of the many individuals that compose it, its nature, its possible role in history, its destiny does not have to be defined elsewhere, on the level of German metaphysics and theology which characterize other problems; they are themselves functions of this praxis too: it is in this praxis that they find the principle of their development. Let us suppose, for example, that this praxis, that is, the activity and effort of living individuals to preserve and increase their life, leads, by the inclusion of material and technological means in it that are more and more powerful, to the following situation, described by Marx under the title of the evolution of productive forces: in the process of production, the part made up of objective elements, that is, the means of production (raw materials and labour instruments), increases continuously, while the share of living labour decreases – so the proletariat, these many working individuals, the sum of this 'living labour', instead of increasing as in the time of Marx and instead of endlessly including new layers of the population, will, on the contrary, decrease too, and eventually disappear. The idea to define the motor and the meaning of human history by living labour would henceforth be empty of meaning.

But from the hypostasis of classes and in particular of the proletariat, another consequence can be drawn that is important to see clearly. As a class considered to be a totality transcendent to the individuals that compose it, as an objective structure, the proletariat, like every reality of this kind, has no thought or will. Nor does it have the capacity to act, if one understands by that effecting a concrete action. One has never seen a society or a social entity digging a hole or building a wall: 'In order to do this,' Marx says, 'one needs men.' If the proletariat as an objective class has to accomplish in history that grand act to which it is called, it cannot in reality be the class that is without consciousness or body – both of which always belong to an individual that will accomplish it – but a group of men who will do all this in its place and in its name. A party – or more precisely, those who are at its head – is the inevitable substitute for the 'worldwide proletariat'.[12] But the party's action on such a large mass of individuals will not be possible except through maintaining a predefined ideology, that is, a concept of a history of the world of which the proletariat is the agent and under which everyone must unite himself, transcending and forgetting himself, in order to fuse into the grand process that, through the dialectic struggle of opposites (proletariat–bourgeoisie), assures the redemption of humanity.

In such a way that everyone no longer finds justification and meaning of his life in himself, in this life that is his own – according to the claim that Marx tirelessly expressed throughout all his philosophical writings – but in the conformity of his action to this movement of history that solely matters, conformity that is indicated to him by the nearest party commissary. In such a way too that the one who refuses to conform to this 'line' which is being carefully traced for him, or who could not do it because of his belonging to the bourgeoisie, which makes of him an exemplary of the 'bourgeois', will have to be eliminated.

In her admirable work *Hope Against Hope*, Nadejda Mandelstam[13] described what she calls 'the ideas of 1920 in Russia', that are in fact those of Leninism, which have replaced, under the name of Marxism, the fundamental philosophical concepts of Marx and yet remain totally ignorant of those. The stirring history of Nadejda and of Ossip Mandelstam – the greatest Russian poet of the century – is only one manifestation among millions of others of the havoc to which these 'ideas' have led, and this in the double form of a political dictatorship and economic bankruptcy. How such a failure, far from being the simple consequence of Marx's own thought, results, on the contrary, from ignorance and incomprehension, is what a brief look at his so-called economic writings will allow us to explain.

Let us first clarify a doubt: Marx's economic theories date precisely from more than a century ago. Are they still capable today of guiding the understanding of the world, infinitely complex, which is ours? Have other theories, more elaborate, born out of contact with new realities, not cast those of Marx in a kind of conceptual death that is the fate of every form of scientific discourse in so far as science is a perpetual surpassing of itself?

What is alive in the economic thought of Marx is precisely the fact that Marx is not an economist in the sense that we normally

understand the term, and that the theoretical corpus which
he has published does not form an economic doctrine among
others, destined like them to be surpassed. Marx is a philosopher
of economy. The initial theme of his research is not the analysis
of economic phenomena, naively taken as such, like a domain
that is previously offered, and in a sense offered of itself for
investigation to the scientist. The fundamental question which
he raises – a properly philosophical question, a transcendental
question – is rather this: How are the economic phenomena in
general possible? What enables something like an economic
reality to emerge at a given moment in the experience of men
and in human history? These are the questions that precede
every *science* of economy, and political economy, because one
cannot analyse economic phenomena in order to discover its
laws if these phenomena did not already exist. So this is the
first, decisive question, but its correlate must not remain hidden,
for the emergence in reality of specific economic phenomena
presents itself as an enigma and as that which needs to be
clarified first of all, only if the original reality is in itself and by
itself nothing economic. And this is precisely Marx's intuition,
rejecting in advance the well-known Marxist–Leninist concepts
that situate the economy at the basis of society and of history as
the substructure on which all the rest is built.

That the original reality is by itself in no way economic is the
result of Marx's philosophical definition of reality as the praxis
of living individuals, that is, as a reality which is that of life itself.
Walking, running, breathing, imagining, thinking, loving, carry
in themselves no economic index at all. One cannot analyse

eroticism but, if one did, one would not find prostitution in it. No more than life, its inorganic correlate, nature, which is worked on in order to make it homogenous as use value – food, clothing, housing and so on – is economic. 'The use value,' Marx says in an essential proposition, 'is not an economic concept of value.'[14] One can analyse a sugar cube but one does not find its price in it. Reality has unfolded itself, living individuals have lived in it and no economic reality has arisen at the horizon of their world. Maybe they will continue to live and no economic reality will exist anymore. The definition of reality as economic reality is what Marx calls fetishism or economic materialism. It is this naïve belief of economists that economic phenomena exist in themselves, and that there is no more to it than to take them as they are in order to investigate them. Yet Marx's analysis is about understanding how a reality which is in itself not economic, 'extra-economic', has been able to become economic. Only if progress is naturally possible in the analysis of economic phenomena and their growing complexity and if, like every scientific theory, economic doctrines are arranged inevitably according to the law of a constant enrichment, then the transcendental genesis of the economic reality from a reality that is not economic in itself is the great discovery of Marx, indifferent to time and to the subsequent insights of political economy: this is what eternally living within Marx's thought means.

The genesis of the economy takes as its starting point in *Capital* the analysis of the commodity. But the commodity is an enigma, at once connected to life as a use value and to economic determination as an exchange value. This must be explained – because 'value does not have its meaning written on its forehead' – or rather its provenance as issuing from a reality that is heterogeneous to it by definition needs to be explained. It is in exchange that use values become exchange values, but exchange – the first historical exchange that brought about an economic reality within the world of men – is itself a mystery, because how can products that differ qualitatively and quantitatively be exchanged? One knows the answer of the English school: different products are susceptible to exchange to the extent that they result from the same labour. Labour, itself measured by the objective time of its duration and by its nature (qualified labour or not) is the unit, the measure, the universal element that, subsuming to itself qualitatively different products, allows overcoming their heterogeneity, establishing an equivalence among them and as such enabling their exchange.

Except that in a philosophy of subjective praxis, *the* labour does not exist. It is nothing objective or universal, no measure for anything other than itself and unable to be measured by anything else. Labour is the irreducibly singular deployment of the power of a body essentially individual, and in this mute accomplishment of the potentialities of organic subjectivity, delivered to the ineffability of its night, it only 'knows' what it is in itself, in its effort and suffering. This is why the temporality of this radically subjective effort has nothing to do with the objective time of the universe and cannot be measured by it either. Also, when in presence of the variety of products brought to the market, one goes back to the labour from which they result, in order to determine their value and be able to exchange them. What is found, then, is not a unity capable of dominating this diversity and reducing it but a more radical diversity, the irreducible diversity of 'real work', that is, the work of isolated bodily monads.

Since one cannot find the measure of the resulting products in the subjective activity of labour and in its subjective temporality, a measure that would enable their exchange, one has to construct this measure and therefore give to this subjective labour, as Marx says, 'a different form than itself',[15] by proposing an objective equivalent. The construction of this objective equivalent of real, subjective labour is the transcendental genesis of economy. It is the construction of what Marx calls 'abstract labour'. And this, by his own definition, is his great discovery: this duplication of labour in living labour on the one hand, and economic labour on the other.[16] This duplication is in its turn a duplication of life and economy, which makes of the latter the simple objective representation of the concrete activities of men. It is an abstract representation in the sense that it abandons all real characteristics of this activity – pain, suffering, effort – substituting for them this ideal 'equivalent', which consists in the idea of skilled or unskilled labour and a quantitative measurement, itself ideal, of its objective duration. The economy is thus not life, retaining none of its vital characteristics, being only the ensemble of quantifiable substitutes by which life is replaced in order to submit it to calculation. This is how Marx's critique of economy is radical: in exchanging the lived determinations of praxis for a relational system of ideal entities, what it accomplishes is nothing less than the substitution of life for death.

However, there is a totally different aspect than a kind of ethical judgement on the level of economy here: the principal of its theoretical explanation. For, if all economic phenomena – exchange value and its pure form: money; its increase: surplus value and capital; its distribution: income, profit, interest – are only ideal representations of the real process of labour and production, then it is evident that they cannot be explained by themselves but by the real process of which they are the double. A fantastic double, from the moment one grants it an effective autonomy: it is then that value seems to increase by itself, and this self-augmentation of exchange value is capital in its various forms. The critique of capital consists in the denunciation of its pretended autonomy and in the unveiling of its illusory character. For the production of value and a fortiori its growth in reality refer to the living labour that produces this value, because the exchange value is the representation in the product of the abstract labour necessary for its production. This abstract labour is in its turn nothing but the representation of the real labour that has accomplished this production. Marx's entire economic problematic, 'the critique of political economy', thus presents itself as an analysis which crosses economic reality in order to go to its source, to its true substance, its real determinants. And every time it seems that these real determinants are not themselves of the economic order, but, under the umbrella of these phenomena and their laws, taken for a specific and independent reality by economists, they are the praxis of living individuals who produce them and continue to do so.

It is to life that we must turn in order to understand the apparent economic phenomena and their variations: surplus value, incomprehensible on the level of pure economy and which explains itself only through this characteristic of life in each individual to produce more use values than those necessary during this production and, as such, more exchange values than the production costs. Yet most of all, it is the conservation of exchange value, essential for every economic system, that refers to what needs to be called a metaphysics, or better, a radical ontology of life. For exchange value cannot be conserved unless the use value, which always supports it, is conserved. But the use value of an object, a fragment of nature, is in its turn only conserved if its form, the form of this object that shapes its use, is itself preserved. This safeguarding of the form of the object, this information of nature which conforms it to life's desire, is the work of life itself, and at the same time its condition. Marx described in poetic terms this original embrace of life and of the world, and how the fragile power of the former, burning fire which twists matter and shapes it to its action, constantly imprints its form into this matter and thereby subjugates it. Moreover, it is this fragile life that, holding the entire nature in the grip of its praxis, properly maintains nature in being, tearing it away from nothingness. For, outside of this grip, from the moment this grip ceases even for an instant, the object loses its form, its utility disappears, the instrument rusts, subsistence withers, harbours silt up, civilizations die.

Let us imagine, then, times in which, by the power of mysterious conditions which we can nevertheless glimpse everywhere, one would have preferred great abstract entities – History, Society, the Proletariat, the Revolution, Central Planning or Bureaucracy which substitutes its proper finalities for those of the individuals[17] – instead of individuals themselves (who alone are carriers of praxis and life). Or else let us imagine that, according to the terrible prophecy of Nietzsche, this life would have turned against itself – giving birth to the disgust of labour, the denigration of talent, doing away with every difference, every form of superiority and invention: then the collapse and drifting of entire societies, particularly those that claim Marxism, would become intelligible in the light of the thought of Marx himself.

To this thought, that assigns to all that is its principle and foundation in life, also belongs the idea of progress, that is not only, according to the idea held dear in the nineteenth century, the progress of science but precisely that of life. Through the effect of scientific and technical progress, of course, but above all because of the proper dynamism of life of which scientific thought is only one form, the process of production is the theatre of a decisive modification to which we have already alluded: the progressive diminishing of living labour, the liberation of life for other tasks. These tasks were, in the eyes of Marx, those of culture. 'Free time' is not a synonym for 'leisure'; life essentially being dynamism, movement, effort, tension and self-transcendence, it could overcome the material process of production only by investing its energies in the highest activities of the mind: theoretical and aesthetical, says the *Critique of the Gotha Programme*. But as the diminution of human effort in the production of human life is accompanied, on the contrary, by the growing passivity of man's existence, surrendered to the media and to imitation, will the times of distress come which Marx's optimism did not anticipate, but which his very lucidity, his 'eagle's eye of thought', of which the letter to his father speaks, sadly makes transparent for us?

What is alive today of the philosophy of Marx is this philosophy itself, as long as one dissociates it from the ideologies and the regimes in which it got lost. What is dead are these ideologies and these regimes, which everywhere in the world are called 'Marxism'.

3

Productive forces and subjectivity

The ultimate contradiction of capitalism, according to Marx, can be understood and must be described as follows[1]: *Capitalism is the system of value, of its development and its maintenance (money, eternal value): value is exclusively produced by living labour; the destiny of capital is thus the destiny of this work, of the subjective praxis of the individual. In as much as the real process of production includes in itself the accomplishment of this praxis, it is identical to a process of formation of value, a process of valorization.*[2] Hence the first moment in the reflection of Marx: the analysis of capital in its effective existence, that is, the analysis of the process of its formation, which leads back to the analysis of the real production process and to the revelation of the element that produces value, subjective praxis. Economic analysis is thus nothing more than the analysis of the effects of the real components of the process; the composition of capital into value refers, as an organic composition, to its technical composition and is explained entirely by it.

If one establishes now a material process of production from which living labour would be excluded, this process is no longer a process of valorization. No system of value results or could result from it, and capitalism is henceforth impossible. The transition from capitalism to socialism is nothing other than the transition from a production process, in which living labour is dominant, to a process in which this part is continuously diminished and eventually annihilated. This is why one can, to the decisive hypothesis of *Capital*, c (constant capital) = 0, oppose (if one wishes to grasp the eidetic cleavage between capitalism and socialism) this other hypothesis, not less *essential* (understood as unveiling an essence): vc (variable capital) = 0. Concretely, we are dealing with a fully automatic system of production in which the products have, despite their quantity and their quality, no value at all. The dissociation in social wealth between real wealth and economic wealth presents itself here in a pure form: an undefined quantity of use values that do not have any exchange value. And this is precisely the theoretical limit, insurmountable, of the market economy and, a fortiori, of capitalism. Marx analysed this movement twice, through which living labour gradually finds itself removed from the process of production. Once on the level of its effects, on the economic level: this is *Capital*. Yet, to the extent that it is an analysis, the 'immanent' law of the tendency of the rate of profit to fall is unequivocally referred to its real *naturans*, to the real process. In the *Grundrisse*, this is the object of an explicit issue. There, an event unfolds itself which will determine modern history, even if this history is yet to come, even if today we are only just aware of it: *the dissociation,*

*at the heart of reality, between the process of production and the
process of labour.*

Such dissociation is undoubtedly present in capitalism, and
long before that, in the elementary forms of human production,
for example in agriculture.[3] If one examines the process that
culminates in the production of grains, that stretches over a
certain amount of months, it is clear that it does not coincide with
the effective human labour that is the condition of it: the labour
is interrupted during the long periods necessary for the grain
to germinate in the soil, for the crop to ripen in the sun and so
on. The same applies, much later, to the industry where the time
to manufacture a product exceeds the labour time because of
inevitable interruptions of the labour – whether due to the
material conditions of the production or to the vital praxis itself
(the necessary time to eat, to rest, to sleep, etc.). Moreover, it
is very remarkable that such a dissociation between the time of
production and the time of labour – and consequently between
production and labour – was taken into consideration by Marx
in the way it was. This is not an otherwise banal and 'contingent'
fact, which he could have taken into account as a factor among
others. It became the principle itself of his analysis. If it is living
labour and only this which produces value, the delimitation of
the subjective accomplishments is equally, in the core of the
production process, the seizure of its *naturans*. This is why,
from the moment there is differentiation between the time of
production and of labour, the presupposition of Marx's thought
is in question: 'The question that concerns us here is that, with an
equal labor time, certain products demand a variable length of

time in order to be completed. One pretends in this case that fixed capital acts alone, *without the help of any living labor,* and one cites the example of a seedling buried in the soil . . . *it is important to ask this question in all its purity.*' We know the answer to it: it is labour and its duration, not that of production, that constitute the principle of value. '*Value, and thus also surplus value, does not equal the duration of the production phase, but the time of labor, materialized and living – spent in the course of this production phase.* Living labor only – used in proportion to materialized labor – can produce surplus value, because it creates time of surplus labor.' That is why, Marx adds, 'It has therefore correctly been asserted that in this regard agriculture, for instance, is less productive (productivity is concerned here with the production of values) than other industries.'[4] If, therefore, the natural conditions create a divergence between the production process and the labour process, only the latter remains as the fundament of valorization. '*The point to remember here* is only that capital creates no surplus value as long as it employs no living labor.'[5] And one can clearly see what must have been the tendency of capital to the extent that it constitutes its own objective: to reduce, where possible, the process of production to the labour process, that is, to a process that is, through and through, a process of valorization. 'Hence the tendency of capitalist production to reduce as much as possible the excess, in terms of time, of the period of production over the labor period.'[6] When the relation of the production process to the labour process obeys a tendency, the tendency of capital to increase indefinitely, and finds itself determined by it, this relation is specific to capitalism. Yet, at this point it becomes contradictory. For if capitalism strives to bring back production to labour, because only the latter is a source of value, it also does the opposite. It is not labour, but surplus labour that founds valourization, it is surplus labour that must be increased. But since the work day is limited – here again it is life that imposes its regulations on economy – increasing the surplus labour amounts to reducing the necessary labour, continuously increasing the productivity, and thus perfecting and developing the technical and instrumental production indefinitely. Far from being reduced to living labour, production seems to be defined by its objective elements and, more and more, obeys them. One thus needs to reread the history of modern industry here.

We have seen how, with the development of machinery, the social forces of production, the skill and cooperation of working individuals, know-how and intelligence cease to be subjective forces, forces and accomplishments of individuals, in order to take place in front of them, under the form of an 'automatic system of machines', which belongs to capital and tends to form the essence of the production process in which individuals are nothing more than scattered auxiliaries, mediocre and too quickly rendered useless. At this point, the decisive transformation of the instrument of labour comes about. It loses its 'immediate form', which is no longer precisely an instrument *of labour*, the means by which praxis communicates its activity to elaborate and fashion the object. 'In the machine . . . the use value, i.e. the material quality of the means of labor, is transformed . . . In no way does the machine appear as the individual worker's means of labor. *Its distinguishing characteristic is not in the least, as with*

the means of labor, to transmit the worker's activity to the object.[7]
The transformation of the nature and the role of the instrument
that has become a machine thus entails, as its consequence,
the decisive transformation by virtue of which *activity is no
longer a fact of the individual, a modality of a vital praxis and
its actualization. On the contrary, paradoxically, activity becomes
that of the machine, an objective process.* 'In reality,' the text we
comment on continues, '*this activity, rather, is posited in such
a way that it merely transmits the machine's work, the machine's
action*, on to the raw material – supervises it and guards against
interruptions. Not as with the instrument, which the worker
animates and makes into his organ with his skill and strength,
and whose handling therefore depends on his virtuosity. Rather,
it is the machine which possesses skill and strength in place of
the worker, is itself the virtuoso, with a soul of its own in the
mechanical laws acting through it.'[8]

One must be careful not to reduce the content of this text
to the anthropological and axiological meaning it conveys:
when the activity that carries within it an ability has ceased to be
the activity of the individual in order to merge with the objective
functioning of the mechanical system, *it is the essence of the
production that has changed: no longer defined by the subjective
praxis, the production process has ceased to be a labour process*,
and here the contradiction of capitalism explodes. As a 'formal
power', capital contained living labour. It lived off living labour; it
fed itself like a vampire, drawing from it the new value by which
it increased; but under the effect of capital itself, which tends
to constantly reduce the necessary labour, living labour finds

itself gradually excluded from the production process that takes on an objective form. It is, at the same time as the subjective accomplishment, the source of value itself which is dried up. 'Capital itself is the moving contradiction, in that it presses to reduce labor time to a minimum, while it posits labor time, on the other side, as the sole measure and source of wealth . . . On the one side, then, it calls to life all the powers of science and of nature, as of social combination and of social intercourse, in order to make the creation of wealth independent . . . of the labor time employed on it. On the other side, it wants to use labor time as the measuring rod for the giant social forces thereby created, and to confine them within the limits required to maintain the already created value *qua* value.'[9] As such, the self-destruction of capital is identical to the historical movement whereby living labour set up as the fundament of value finds itself excluded from the production process. The production process and the labour process thus continue to diverge.

Is socialism, then, different from the consequences of this contradiction or, put theoretically, the awareness of it? What is prescribed by the theorists of socialism is the suppression of the market economy and of capitalism, but only to the extent that socialism has brought the market economy to the point where it has become contradictory. Yet this prescription is nothing but a finding; it follows immediately from the suppression. If one no longer needs to conceive of the wealth of a society as economic wealth, if one no longer needs to define the value of a product on the basis of its exchange value, it is because this value is only the theoretical account of the living labour needed for the production of this product. It is, ultimately, because living labour has precisely disappeared, or tends to disappear from this production. We do not condemn market economy, we assist its demise. And in the collapse of the universe of economic wealth arises, in all its purity, the collapse of real wealth defined by use values. It is a fact, once again, that those values proliferate when their exchange value tends to reach zero. The progression of real wealth at the expense of economic wealth is simply the correlate of the decisive change that affects the production process and, in this process, substitutes living labour by mechanical manufacture.

It is thus the concept of 'productive forces' that must eventually be fully investigated. One says all too often that the productive forces are the determining process in a society from which, eventually, everything can be explained: 'social relations', ideology and so on. We have demonstrated how, in this superficial summary, Marx's thought is already lost. For it consists precisely in the analysis of productive forces, in the distribution made in them of the objective element and living praxis. The entire economic analysis rests on this distribution. The decisive mutation of the concept of productive forces – and the result of it: the passage from capitalism to socialism – means that henceforth the distribution is made differently. Now one must understand, importantly, that this is a change that upsets the history of humankind. As long as the determining element of production is the subjective activity, *production coincides with the life of individuals*, its essence is their vital process and, conversely, what individuals are is what they do to produce the necessary supplies for their survival: it is their 'material' production. The subjective definition of production has this double meaning, contains this double reduction: the reduction of the production to the individual way of life, to the conditions of human existence, and the reduction of this life to what they make in this production, to this production itself. Such is the explicit content of one of the fundamental texts which opens *The German Ideology*: 'The way in which men produce their means of subsistence depends first of all on the nature of the means of subsistence they actually find in existence and have to reproduce. This mode of production must not be considered simply as being the reproduction of the physical existence of the individuals. *Rather it is a definite form of activity of these individuals, a definite form of expressing their life, a definite mode of life on their part. As individuals express their life, so they are. What they are, therefore, coincides with their production* [Was sie sind, fällt also zusammen mit ihrer Produktion].'[10]

It is thus this subjective essence of the productive forces which will be abolished when they are constituted, not only by what they are but by what they do, like an ensemble of elements foreign to praxis, like an objective process. Let us remember Marx's words: 'It belongs to the concept of capital that the increased productive force of labor is posited rather *as the increase of a force* [Kraft] *outside itself, and as labor's own debilitation* [Entkräftung].'[11] 'Thus, the specific mode of working here appears directly as becoming transferred from the worker to capital in the form of the machine.'[12] 'The increase of the productive force of labor and the greatest possible negation of necessary labor is the necessary tendency of capital ... The transformation of the means of labor into machinery is the realization of this tendency. In machinery, objectified labor materially confronts living labor as a ruling power.'[13] This transformation, in which we easily recognize the dialectic of dead labour and living labour – taken, it is true, not as the element of a system but as its future and as the movement of history itself –this transformation is the one by which the productive force stops being defined by subjectivity in order to find its reality, its 'force', in the objective instrumental mechanism of production and in what Marx calls objective labour. Here, this insight is formulated in a categorical way: 'In machinery, objectified labor itself appears not only in the form of product or of the product employed as means of labor, *but in the form of the force of production itself*.'[14] It is only in light of these essential analyses of the *Grundrisse* that the texts of *Capital* can be fully understood. These texts, in the guise of, once again, anthropological considerations, inasmuch as they seem to deplore the progressive exclusion of the individual abilities and of the individual himself from the process of production, in reality only reaffirm the ontological mutation of productive forces. Indeed, one must understand very well that the 'collective labour force', the 'social productive forces', in short the 'productive forces' as they exist in the way that they have evolved because of capitalism, are no longer able to refer to individual activities even if they are social in their very essence, even if human labour is always co-labour. Because they are now the forces of the machine, productive forces *are no longer the praxis*, no longer the 'forces', in the sense of the potentials and the actualizations of the organic subjectivity and, in general, of life. *They are no longer the 'labour force' in the sense of* Capital, *and the proof of it is that they no longer create any value.*

The 'productive forces of capital', it is true, continue to produce value, although this production seems to be more and more difficult. That is because the concept of 'productive force of capital' remains unclear and, eventually, is no longer usable. One must distinguish within the generic concept of productive forces, between on the one hand, the objective 'forces' of capital, the 'social', 'collective' forces of labour, which are not 'labour', or 'labour forces', which are neither social nor collective – sociality and collectivity are not more than, and cannot be more than modalities of life – which only refer to a coherent, instrumental totality and its objective functioning. And on the other hand, there are the individual forces that belong to life, that can be social and collective, that have been but are no longer (to the extent that the labourers are now dispersed to diverse points of the mechanical system) connected to the system but not to each other. These are the individual forces, and only they produce the value produced by the 'productive forces of capital'. These forces, among which the individual forces are constantly present, produce the use values. The regret provoked by the decline of the role of the individual in capitalist production is not the nostalgic expression of a long-forgone humanism. Rather, it expresses an observation, that of the progressive shift between the subjective forces that create the economic wealth and the objective forces that produce the ever-bigger mass of use values. Without the differentiation of the concept of wealth in its correlation with the internal ontological differentiation of the productive forces, one cannot understand a word from this passage of *Capital*: 'In manufacture, in order to make the *collective laborer, and through him capital, rich in social productive power*, each laborer must be made poor in *individual productive powers*.'[15] And the following quote would also be hard to understand, when Marx declares, considering the productive forces in their connection to the division of labour in the factory: 'It increases the *social productive power of labor . . . for the benefit of the capitalist* instead of for that of the laborer.'[16]

However, what happens when the productive forces cease to be constituted in their very essence by subjectivity and become objective? This is where the market economy, as we know, and with it capitalism are most deeply struck. *Is this not also the case for the philosophy of praxis?* Does not the decline of capitalism also mean the decline of Marx's thought? What is left of the interpretation of being as production *and as subjectivity* when, identifying itself with the mechanical, instrumental devices, production is nothing else than its functioning and, as such, an objective process in the third person? And is not the individual, together with the praxis that defines him, removed from the problematic, that is, from the concept of being as production? Marx has described what happens to the individual in this 'passage' from capitalism to socialism, that is, in the becoming objective of the productive forces, a becoming that, in eliminating its subjective source, ruins the exchange value: 'With that, production based on exchange value breaks down, and the direct, material production process is stripped of the form of penury and antithesis. *This is the free development of individualities*, and hence not the reduction of necessary labor time so as to posit surplus labor, but rather the general reduction of the necessary labor of society to a minimum, *which then corresponds to the artistic, scientific, etc. development of the individuals* in the time set free, and with the means created, for all of them.'[17] The decline of the subjective concept of the productive forces actually marks a turning point in the history of humanity. It expresses the fact that the union between the individual and the production, the definition of his life by the material tasks that assure the maintenance of this life, the 'labour' in the sense in which it has been understood for millennia, ceases to exist. What arises then is the 'free development of individuality'. The individual activity, life and praxis are not abolished, they are restored to their essential state. Activity is no longer determined by material production – this means it is no longer confounded with it and, for this reason, it is no longer doubled by an economic universe. Two things constantly connected, up until the point that they are being confounded, will cut themselves loose and will follow their own paths: production, delivered to technology, becomes a natural process; and life can finally be what it is. Life is experience in itself and finds its goal in its own reality: in itself. The philosophy of the radical development of the individual and of the total individual is thus not a remnant of the humanist anthropology of Marx's youth; it is, at the end of the economic analysis, both its result and a prophecy. The subjective definition of production is presented in *The German Ideology* as being a part of the 'premises' that constitute 'the first premise of all human history';[18] and this is how the definition has been understood in our research, as the transcendental condition of both history and society. Such a definition of history remained dependant both on the actual state of civilization and on its millennial past, for which it is adequate. The history that follows – that will follow – from the market economy is therefore no less the history of individuals, the history of their lives; in a sense, it is what it will be for the first time. It will not be their history as in the history of their lives, but because this history of their life will still be 'wanted' by this life, in accordance with the most personal and interior virtualities of living subjectivity. It will no longer be the history of 'material' needs, but of their 'spiritual' needs.

The interpretation of socialism as a becoming and actualization in the individual existence of its proper ideology permanently erases the aberrant meanings that traditionally cover its concept in Marxism and in common-sense thinking. According to this, socialism would indicate a mutation in the 'history of humanity', the establishment of a new state that could be characterized as 'social'. This has to be understood in the sense of a revolution taking place within being itself. It is reality that would be changed and that, no longer defined by the anarchic plurality of separated individuals delivered to competition, would find itself constituted, on the contrary, as a general reality, in a substantial manner. In the same way that production is no longer individual but social, consisting in the implementation of an immense collective force, so the life of individuals should transcend itself beyond its meaningless particularity. Their activity should be founded in an activity in which all participate, and that is precisely everybody's activity, a 'social praxis'. When, simulated by capital itself, production has become social and deploys its forces without limits; it draws the horizon of the future itself. It is already the honour of everyone to no longer lend to his or her activity the derisory goals of individuality, but to those of history, and to blend within this grand movement. Human beings, who no longer live from themselves, nor for themselves, but who, as modest as their own position and the share they have in the factory or the community's adventure may be, define themselves only by history and by the revolution. These political human beings are indeed the precursors of this state in which everyone lives from an aggrandized life, a life which is no longer theirs but that of the universal reality in which he or she can participate and which is realized through this participation. Everything thus becomes collective, the production that brings about this new world and, consequently, life itself, the relations, thought, objects. Here is the age of groups and teams, of community in all its forms. The individual is among the people like a fish in the water – it can only have its substance within the social substance.

Only, the metaphysics of the universal is Hegel's, of which we have demonstrated that it falls to pieces in Marx's problematics. Already in the manuscript of 1842, the attempt to repeat, with the Feuerbachian concept of the genre and on the level of the civil society, the political definition of individual life as universal life contradicts the arrangement of the elements that guide the later development of Marx's thought. The irreducible nature of individual activity immediately got rid of the ontological pretensions of objective universality. In Marx's later works, it is true, and more precisely when it concerns socialism, certain obscurities have given rise to serious misinterpretations of which the most important is without a doubt the definition of socialism as something 'social'. This is the case in a series of texts, in which the market economy is condemned for only having established the 'social' under the form of a mediation, that is, in the form of exchange value. We are talking, as one will remember, about the process in which one replaces the real and always particular labour of different individuals by the general and social labour that is supposed to be the common norm that represents them all equally and represents itself in exchange value. 'Labor which manifests itself in exchange value appears to be the labor of an isolated individual. It becomes social labor by assuming the form of its direct opposite, of abstract universal.'[19] These analyses are not marginal. They describe nothing less than the constitution of the market economy in its own possibility, which we have called its transcendental genesis. We have seen that it is the representation in all works of one and the same work that grants to their products a value and allows for their exchange. However, insofar as, in the market economy, the social appears only in the form of a general and abstract labour opposed to real labour of the individuals, that is, to their effective existence, that which has to constitute the bond between all the existences and their substance, precisely the social factor, reveals itself alien to immediate life: it is beyond this life, in unreality, where it unfolds its reign, in a fantastic universe by which existence will continue to be affected.

Only when the question of socialism in Marx's work is not the object of an explicit thematic – this is almost never the case – but the object of remarks or meaningful surveys, it is the most original presupposition of the market economy that inevitably presents itself to thought. It then appears that the labour from which the process of alienation originates, which grounds social labour and exchange value is not only, as has been said, the real labour of individuals, but also *private* labour. 'Only particular commodities, the particular use values embodying the labor of private individuals, confront one another in the exchange process.'[20] It is because the labour that is taken into account in exchange, and in reality is exchanged by it, is first private labour, presented as such at the start of the economic process, that it can only be dressed up with a social form when stripping itself from its primitive character, alienating itself, that *the 'social' will appear not as a given and at the level of immediate life but as the result of this process of alienation, in an abstract and unreal form.*

> *The point of departure is not the labor of individuals considered as social labor but on the contrary the particular kinds of labor of private individuals, i.e., labor which proves that it is universal social labor only by the supersession of its original character in the exchange process. Universal social labor is consequently not a ready-made prerequisite.*[21]

The 'solution' of socialism – of what seems to be Marx's socialism – thus lies before us. It consists in the opposite presupposition to that of the market economy, the presupposition according to which the individual labour, that certainly constitutes the essence and the condition of all possible production, also and immediately constitutes social labour. What is presupposed here is *the becoming effective of the social substance*, the fact that it is henceforth merged with the life of people instead of being lost beyond this life in the unreality of abstraction – *as if the bond which unites the individuals could be separated from each of them*. This is precisely the paradox of market economy. However, the presupposition of socialism is not a simple presupposition in the sense of a moral postulation. It is, in the language of *The German Ideology*, a 'real presupposition', and Marx has no difficulty showing that it has been effective in history and, in a way, does not cease to be effective in each moment. It is what is produced in the family – provided that it is not a worker family from Manchester – where each individual's labour is immediately 'social' labour, which does not have to split itself ideally in order to acquire a property it already has on the level of reality. Consequently, this product does not have any economic value and is not exchanged, but naturally takes its place in the ensemble of the use values put at the disposal of all the members of this family, for everyone according to his or her needs. In the primitive society, too, 'the social character of labor is evidently not effected by the labor of the individual assuming the abstract form of universal labor or his product assuming the form of a universal equivalent. *The communal system on which this mode of production is based prevents the labor of an individual from becoming private labor and his product the private product of a separate individual*.'[22]

The solution that socialism proposes thus takes the form of the community characterized by *the transparency of the social relations*.[23]

But how is the community, which brings the social relations to life and the individual to himself, possible? It has already been said that this is on the condition that individual labour is immediately social labour. In the *Grundrisse*, a project announcing a work on history says, 'Dissolution of the mode of production and the form of society grounded in exchange value. The individual labor posed actually under a social form, and vice versa.' On the presupposition of individual labour as social labour, to the extent that it defines the actual presupposition of socialism, the *Grundrisse* adds important specifications. They demonstrate how only *labour that is in itself general* can avoid the mediation of exchange and the exchange value: 'On the basis of exchange values, labor is posited as general only through exchange. But on this foundation it would be posited as such before exchange; i.e. the exchange of products would in no way be the medium by which the participation of the individual in the general production is mediated.'[24] But is not labour subjective, and, as such, particular and not general? Speaking about labour as a 'subjective form of activity', Marx adds, 'It is by no means general, self-equivalent labor time.'[25] Only a mediation can lead from individual, subjective activity to general labour. In socialism, this mediation is immediate: it consists in the fact that activity, in itself singular and lived as such, is not less placed and grasped, in its own accomplishment, as a part of the collective activity in which it always fits. In this way, individual labour is nevertheless 'general', not in the form of an ideal double, but in its reality, insofar, once more, as it is not understood as 'private', explicitly and judicially referred to a given individual, but as a personal and active participation in the common activity, while constituting this activity.

> Mediation must, of course, take place. In the first case, which proceeds from the independent production of individuals – no matter how much these independent productions determine and modify each other post festum through their interrelations – mediation takes place through the exchange of commodities, through the exchange value and through money; all these are expressions of one and the same relation. In the second case, the presupposition is itself mediated; i.e. a communal production, communality, is presupposed as the basis of production. The labor of the individual is posited from the outset as social labor.[26]

Like this labour, its product too is social, and not private. Moreover, because the totality of the products is the correlate of a collective production, it is not a given product that could be related to individual labour, and eventually attributed to it, but a part of the collective product of this social production. Immediately after this, the text says, 'Whatever the particular material form of the product he [the individual] creates or helps to create, what he has bought with his labor is not a specific and particular product, but rather a specific share of the communal production.'[27] In the same passage, one reads,

> The communal character of production would make the product into a communal, general product from the outset.

The exchange which originally takes place in production – which would not be an exchange of exchange values but of activities, determined by communal needs and communal purposes – would from the outset include the participation of the individual in the communal world of products.

Here is the crux of communitarian socialism – of what Marx calls communism. If one can understand how a labour, in itself individual, is nevertheless inscribed in a process of collective production, as a real part of it – 'The participation of the individual in the collective world of products' – this is nothing else than its consumption, that essentially remains individual. The participation of the individual means nothing other than a reality, in itself singular, which is grounded in a totality that goes beyond it but, entirely opposed to a totality of goods, is divided into a certain number of parts that must be attributed to different individuals. It is the principle of this distribution that cannot be eluded. The latter no longer rests on the fact that the products are merchandises and that they are obtained in exchange for a certain quantity of money. What is exchanged in socialism, Marx tells us, are immediately individual activities of the workers, in the act by which they are constituent of one and the same social production of which the different branches and, eventually, the multiple labours they imply, are complementary and destined to form a global wealth adequate for all human needs. *In market economy, however, the exchange of products called merchandises, in accordance with their value, is nothing else than the exchange of individual labour as represented by this value.* Moreover – and like in 'socialist economy' – this exchange of individual labour is what is accomplished first. It is only because at the outset of the process the particular activity of each individual at work is immediately counted as social labour that the product has value, that is, the representation of this part of *social labour* it contains. It is thus entirely wrong to oppose, as Marx does, the market economy, where exchange is supposed to rest – post festum – only on value, to the socialist economy in which it directly concerns the particular activities of individuals working towards collective goals. Marx's analysis teaches us that the exchange of merchandises was not original but rather a secondary phenomenon that refers, in its founding possibility, to this act of representing individual labour immediately as social labour, that is, to the substitution of abstract labour for real labour. In this substitution, which replaces subjectivity for ideality, resides the alienation constitutive of the market economy.

Is such alienation absent from socialist economy? In no way. When it is a matter of fixing the part of the social and 'collective' wealth that returns to each worker, it is his own, individual work that is taken into account. Counting labour when the subjective praxis is beyond measure, is substituting it by a system of objective and ideal equivalents, it is counting the labour *time*. What the immediate position of individual labour as social labour means must be made clear. Either it means that the real praxis is inscribed in a collective production – but then one must recognize that this is always the case, in market economy as well as in socialist economy. Or it means the quantitative and qualitative norm whereby the praxis is subsumed for its definition and thus its retribution, the substitution of individual labour by general social labour, and then one must recognize that this substitution exists both in socialist economy and in market economy. Marx wanted to make us understand what the redistribution of a social wealth could be.

> Let us now picture to ourselves, by way of change, a community of free individuals, carrying on their work with the means of production in common, in which the labor power of all the different individuals is consciously applied *as* the combined labor power of the community . . . The total product of our community is a *social* product. One portion serves as a fresh means of production and remains social. But another portion is consumed by the members as means of subsistence . . . We will assume, but merely for the sake of a parallel with the production of commodities, that the share of each individual producer in the means of subsistence is determined by his *labor time*. Labor time would, in that case, play a double part. Its apportionment in accordance with a definite social plan maintains the proper proportion between the different kinds of work to be done and the various wants of the community. On the other hand, it also serves as a measure of the portion of the common labor borne by each individual, and of his share in the part of the total product destined for individual consumption.[28]

In exchange for a certain *labour time*, the worker in market economy receives a certain sum of money; in a socialist economy he receives 'labour vouchers' – money or vouchers with which he can acquire a certain number of products. The question is thus the following: *Are labour vouchers different than money?* In a passage in volume two of *Capital*, which demonstrates the permanent element in every production, whatever the social form of it is, and in the occurrence of the long or short duration of a determined production to the extent that the production depends on the material nature of its components, Marx finds that

> under socialized as well as capitalist production, the laborers in branches of business with shorter working periods will as before withdraw products only for a short time without giving any products in return; while branches of business with long working periods continually withdraw products for a longer time before they return anything.[29]

This reveals the problem of this 'setting aside', from the perspective of the workers, for the social wealth. 'The producers,' the text continues, 'can receive vouchers in exchange for which they can collect at the social consumer deposits, a quantity corresponding to their labor time. These vouchers are not money. They do not circulate.' But vouchers given in exchange for certain products circulate. When Marx says that these vouchers do not circulate, he has in mind not circulation sensu stricto, the exchange of equivalents, but the capitalist circulation in which money is exchanged for labour instruments and for labour itself, which increases the surplus value and thus becomes capital. 'Capital money disappears in socialist production,' is said in a sentence immediately preceding the above quote.

Let us remember that Marx's critique of the market economy is double: it is first a critique of capitalism, the exposure of the origins of surplus value in surplus labour. But the alienation in question here is no longer capitalist alienation; it is the alienation proper to the market economy as such and, despite certain Marxist declarations, this alienation exists in socialist regimes, in fact within communism. Once the praxis is taken up in the social, from the moment it is represented, either in a labour voucher or in money, what constitutes it substantially as proper each time to a specific individual and as identical to his existence is removed: the substitution of life for an ideal equivalent is effective. Capitalism covers up this fundamental alienation with another. Communism exhibits such alienation in its pure form. This was precisely the content of the *Critique of the Gotha Programme*. The decisive problematic of equal rights has shown the principal impossibility of producing an economic formula adequate to life.

It is thus useless to affirm that production is immediately social if the account taken of the individual is inevitable on the level of consumption as it is on the level of production, if the part of the social wealth due to each person results and must result from his labour. Far from finding a definition through the becoming social of this process in the modern industry, through the social or collective character of their management, socialism maintains only an extrinsic relation with its determinations with which it is too often identified. And this in a triple sense, because these determinations constituted for Marx only the historical condition of socialism; because, far from being based on its internal principle and being able to result from it, these determinations are strange to it; because, for these two reasons, the world they unfold is not a socialist world.

One must thus, instead of continuing surreptitiously confound them, oppose socialism and communism, as Marx did in the *Critique of the Gotha Programme*. To the extent that he relies on the socialization of the production process and draws the consequences from it: socialization of the means of production, of the management and so on, communism, we have seen, cannot bypass the problems of the individual, the problem of consumption and of 'labour'. If he tries to reject the alienation constitutive of capitalism, the exploitation of man in surplus labour, he does not abolish the fundamental alienation of the market economy, the becoming different of the real praxis in 'social labour'. Indeed, it is this latter alienation that is targeted by socialism that Marx wanted to eliminate. *He could not do this by substituting the universality of a social essence for the activity of the individual if the alienation consists precisely in such a substitution, if this activity is, on the contrary, what must be restored to itself and liberated.* This is the unequivocal content of the *Critique of the Gotha Programme*. The society of overabundance is not defined by the sum of the social goods that it provides for everyone but, in a decisive and explicit way, by the fact that in such a society the praxis of the individual only yields to himself and to the specific potentialities of life in him.

Such a situation results from the evolution of the productive forces – not from their simple linear development and their increase, as if, more and more 'powerful', they offered an ever-greater wealth to social consumption. *It is the structural modification of their inner ontological constitution alone that enables and explains what Marx understands by a society of overabundance.* It is only when the objective element represented by the instrumental and technological disposition increases within these forces until it merges with them and defines them, that living praxis becomes strange to them, is finally 'free', and is stricto sensu an activity *of the individual.* Then the absolutely new historical situation is realized – will be realized – in which the life of men will no longer be confused, as it has been for millennia, with their 'material' life, that is, with the production of the necessary goods for their needs. Then will be born their new need, the need of their own activity as such and as living activity, as the *activity of their life.*

When the concept of socialism leaves the mists of Marxist ideology and logomachy, the socialization of the means of production and its most usual results – shortage on the material level, bureaucracy and the police – can decidedly no longer represent its content. What is being proposed today, the self-management of the worker, is not less alien to Marx's fundamental project: the first one (the socialization of the means of production) aims at making the individual activity and the production possible together at the same time, the second (the worker's self-management) presupposes their progressive divergence and eventually their absolute separation. Without a doubt, this only defines an ideal limit and, as long as the production will imply in itself at least the partial maintenance of the living labour, the question whether to keep the 'human' form for this labour will inevitably be posed. This preoccupation is, by the way, constant in Marx's thought. It governs not only the entire critique of the condition of the worker in capitalism, but manifests itself also, in a positive way, in a good many aspects of the doctrine and, for example, in the theory of education. Indeed, one can only prescribe that education 'in the case of every child over a given age, combine productive labor with instruction and gymnastics, not only as one of the methods of adding to the efficiency of production, but as the only method of producing fully developed human beings'.[30] One can do this only if the immanence of the individual activity to the production, the 'labour', remains caught in the sight of the problematic. The preponderant influence that had the ideas of Owen on these developments forbid us to see in them the pure product of Marx's thought. This, rather, is only fully expressed through the singular overthrow that emerges in the above-quoted text. Because it is no longer for the production that the individual, even the adolescent, has to participate, but only in order to actualize the practical potentialities of his own subjectivity, whether this actualization is inserted in a social production or not. In any case, socialism rests upon principal questions. If the exclusion of the living labour outside of the social production belongs to its concept, the thematic that concerns this exclusion and its prescriptions – socialization, auto-management and so on – have only a secondary role, an extrinsic meaning. Socialist can only be said about (1) a society of overabundance, (2) in which the living praxis is no longer busy with production. The connection which unites these two fundamental meanings of the concept of socialism is, by the way, evident if the 'surplus' does not mean anything else, eventually, than the 'freedom' of the praxis.

In the concept of socialism is inscribed a second connection, no less essential, which unites socialism and capitalism and shows that the former derives from the latter. The project of the pretention to pass directly from the Middle Ages to the 21st century, or to go to socialism without passing through capitalism does not have a place in the problematic of Marx, nor can it refer to it, if the reciprocal exclusion of the subjectivity and the production, where socialism finds its concept, is the fact of capitalism and its contradiction. The essential connection of overabundance and freedom that defines socialism is precisely nothing other than the historical form developed from the contradiction, inherent to capitalism, of production and subjectivity.

Because economic analysis is rooted in the ultimate structure of being and is determined by it, it draws from this origin the principle and the secret of its radiance and of the strange power with which it reaches us still today. For this reason too, it cannot be included in a memorandum of economic doctrines. The principal fact is that the thought of Marx dominates history. Whether subjectivity forms the essence of production or whether, in a future socialist universe, it will withdraw and be restored to itself, subjectivity constitutes in any case the basis and the unique theme of conceptual development. Marx's thought confronts us with the abyss of the question: What is life?

Notes

Foreword

1 Pagination refers to the current book.

2 *Capital* I, p. 186.

3 *Capital* I, p. 7 (preface to the first German edition). Translation modified. Emphasis in original.

4 *The German Ideology* III, p. 359. Translation modified.

Translator's Note

1 Michel Henry, *Marx: A Philosophy of Human Reality*, translated by Kathleen McLaughlin (Bloomington: Indiana University Press, 1983).

2 Michel Henry, *From Communism to Capitalism: Theory of a Catastrophe*, translated by Scott Davidson (London: Continuum, 2014).

3 Michel Henry, *Barbarism*, translated by Scott Davidson (London: Continuum, 2012).

1 Marx: An introduction

1 Michel Henry, 'Introduction à la pensée de Marx', *Revue Philosophique de Louvain* 67, 3rd series, n° 94, May 1969, 241–266. First translated into English by Daniel Vaillancourt and published as Michel Henry, 'Introduction to the Thought of Marx', *Philosophy Today* 15/3 (1971), 186–203.

2 *The German Ideology I*, p. 31.

3 *The Holy Family*, p. 79.

4 Ibid., p. 93. Emphasis is that of the translator.

5 Translated into English by K. Justaert. Henry's reference is Karl Marx, *L'Idéologie allemande*, translated into French by Karl Molitor (Paris: Editions Costes, 1948), p. 211; translated by Gilbert Badia (Paris: Editions Sociales, 1977), p. 384.

6 *The German Ideology III*, p. 359 (translation modified).

7 *The German Ideology I*, p. 82.

8 *The German Ideology III*, p. 378. Emphasis in original.

9 *The German Ideology III*, p. 206.

10 *The German Ideology III*, p. 214.

11 *The German Ideology I*, p. 99 (translation modified).

12 *The German Ideology III*, p. 342

13 Louis Althusser, *For Marx*, translated by Ben Brewster (London: Allen Lane, 1969), p. 223.

14 Althusser, *For Marx*, p. 227.

15 See Georges Cottier, *L'Athéisme du jeune Marx. Ses origines hégéliennes* (Paris: Vrin, 1959); Georges Cottier, *Du romantisme au marxisme* (Paris: Alsatia, 1961).

16 *The German Ideology I*, p. 37.

17 *Capital I*, p. 270.

18 Translated into English by K. Justaert. Henry refers to Karl Marx, *Grundrisse I*, translated by Dangeville (Paris: Editions Anthropos), p. 450.

19 *The German Ideology I*, p. 45.

20 *Capital I*, p. 368 and p. 366 (translation modified).

21 *Grundrisse*, p. 872.

22 *Capital I*, p. 188.

23 Translated into English by K. Justaert. Henry refers to Karl Marx, *Grundrisse II*, translated by Dangeville, p. 456.

24 Translated into English by K. Justaert. Henry refers to Karl Marx, *Le Capital I*, p. 735, in Karl Marx, *Oeuvres complètes, Tome I* (Bibliothèque de la Pléiade, Paris: Gallimard).

25 Translated into English by K. Justaert. Henry refers to Karl Marx, *Grundrisse II*, translated by Dangeville, p. 105.

26 *Grundrisse*, p. 272.

27 *Grundrisse*, p. 611. In the footnote accompanying this quote, *grisette* is defined as 'young shop-girl'.

28 Translated into English by K. Justaert. Henry refers to Karl Marx, *Oeuvres complètes* I, p. 570.

29 Translated into English by K. Justaert. Henry refers to Karl Marx, *Oeuvres complètes* I, *Lettre à Annenkov* (28 December 1846), p. 1444.

30 Translated into English by K. Justaert. Henry refers to Karl Marx, *Grundrisse II*, translated by Dangeville, p. 34.

31 *Grundrisse*, p. 171.

32 *Grundrisse*, p. 171 (emphasis M. Henry).

33 *Capital I*, p. 51.

34 *Grundrisse*, p. 168.

35 *Grundrisse*, p. 171.

36 Karl Marx and Friedrich Engels, *Capital I*, translated by Samuel Moore
and Edward Aveling (New York: International Publishers, 1967), p. 166.

37 *Grundrisse*, p. 641.

38 *Capital I*, p. 186.

2 Life, death: Marx and Marxism

1 Extract of 'Diogène', n° 125, January–March 1984. First translated into
English by R. Scott Walker and published as Michel Henry, 'Life and
Death: Marx and Marxism', *Diogenes* 32/125 (1984), 115–132.

2 *The German Ideology I*, p. 31.

3 Karl Marx, *The Poverty of Philosophy* (New York: International
Publishers, 1963), p. 92.

4 *The German Ideology*, p. 359.

5 *The German Ideology*, p. 436–437.

6 See note 5 of Chapter 1. Translated into English by K. Justaert.
Henry's reference is Karl Marx, *L'Idéologie allemande*, translated
into French by Karl Molitor (Paris: Editions Costes, 1948), p. 211;
translated by Gilbert Badia (Paris: Editions Sociales, 1977), p. 384.

7 K. Marx, *A Contribution to the Critique of Political Economy*
(Moscow: Progress Publishers, 1977), preface (see https://www.
marxists.org/archive/marx/works/1859/critique-pol-economy/
preface.htm).

8 *The Eighteenth Brumaire of Louis Bonaparte*, p. 239–240.

9 Whatever its power, a modern society's ideological conditioning of
its members is thus only a secondary phenomenon and, by the way,
always secretly dependent on a conditioning by the way of life itself,
as is shown by the inevitable fall, one day or another, of all ideologies.

10 I [Michel Henry] have shown elsewhere that this expression, to which Marx's thought on history is roughly reduced, has no empirical or factual meaning whatsoever. It concerns a certain segment of past human history and in no way constitutes the condition of all possible history, and even less the principle of this history. If the 'historical materialism' is proposed as the theory of the principle of all history, the theory of class struggle is not a part of it. See Michel Henry, *Marx, I, Une philosophie de la réalité, II, Une philosophie de l'économie*, I, Chapitre III (Paris: Gallimard, 1976). Note of translator: this work has been translated into English in an abbreviated form by Kathleen McLaughlin as Michel Henry, *Marx: A Philosophy of Human Reality* (Bloomington: Indiana University Press, 1983).

11 *Critique of Hegel's Philosophy of Right*, translated by Joseph O'Malley, www.marxists.org, p. 10.

12 Maximilien Rubel correctly denounced the replacement of the proletariat, which Marx called a people, by a party, and later, a State which the party captures and to which it grants a totalitarian character (cf. Maximilien Rubel, *Marx, critique du marxisme* (Paris: Payot, 1974)). That this great scholar, from a historical, sociological and political perspective (and as such different from our essentially philosophical approach) reaches these conclusions often analogous to ours, and particularly the insight in the opposition between Marx's thought and Marxism, is all the more significant.

13 N. Mandelstam, *Hope against Hope: A Memoir*, translated by Max Hayward (Harmondsworth: Penguin Books, 1975).

14 *Grundrisse*, p. 872.

15 *Grundrisse*, p. 171.

16 The double character of commodities as use value and exchange value is only the consequence of the prior duplication of work and its reflection in the commodity.

17 One finds in the *Critique of Hegel's Doctrine of the State* an implacable denunciation of bureaucracy; the regimes in which bureaucracy is insanely developed cannot, in this regard as well, claim to descend from Marx.

3 Productive forces and subjectivity

1 Extract of 'Diogène', n° 88, October–December 1974. First translated
    into English by Simon Pleasance and published as Michel Henry,
    'Productive Forces and Subjectivity: Socialism as Marx Saw It',
    Diogenes 22/88 (1974), 77–99.

2 See Michel Henry, *Marx. Tome I: Une philosophie de la réalité;
    tome II: Une philosophie de l'économie* (Paris: Gallimard, 1976).
    An abridged version of this work has been translated into English
    by Kathleen McLaughlin as *Marx: A Philosophy of Human Reality*
    (Bloomington: Indiana University Press, 1983). Emphasis in original.

3 *Grundrisse*, p. 603.

4 *Grundrisse*, p. 669 (emphasis M. Henry).

5 Grundrisse, p. 670 (emphasis M. Henry).

6 *Capital II*, translated by Samuel Moore and Edward Aveling, p. 124.

7 *Grundrisse*, p. 692 (emphasis M. Henry).

8 *Grundrisse*, p. 692–693 (emphasis M. Henry).

9 *Grundrisse*, p. 607 (translation modified).

10 *The German Ideology*, p. 31 (emphasis M. Henry).

11 *Grundrisse*, p. 702 (emphasis M. Henry).

12 *Grundrisse*, p. 704.

13 *Grundrisse*, p. 693.

14 *Grundrisse*, p. 694 (emphasis M. Henry).

15 *Capital I*, translated by Moore and Aveling, p. 361 (emphasis
    M. Henry).

16 *Capital I*, translated by Moore and Aveling, p. 364.

17 *Grundrisse*, p. 705–706 (emphasis M. Henry).

18 *The German Ideology*, p. 81.

19 *The Critique of Political Economy*, p. 34 (emphasis M. Henry).

20 *The Critique of Political Economy*, p. 45.

21 *The Critique of Political Economy*, p. 45 (emphasis M. Henry).

22 *The Critique of Political Economy*, p. 33–34 (emphasis M. Henry). It is precisely because the social character of labour is understood by him as original that Marx conceives of private labour and private property as the historical effect and the result of the dissolution of the primitive mode of production: 'A careful study of Asiatic, particularly Indian, forms of communal property would indicate that the disintegration of different forms of primitive communal ownership gives rise to diverse forms of property' (ibid., p. 33). Likewise, in the *Grundrisse* we find, 'The system of production founded on private exchange is, to begin with, the historic dissolution of this naturally arisen communism' (p. 882).

23 An exposition on the 'community' was not possible in the context of this extract.

24 *Grundrisse*, p. 171.

25 *Grundrisse*, p. 171.

26 *Grundrisse*, p. 171–172.

27 *Grundrisse*, p. 172.

28 *Capital I*, translated by Moore and Aveling, p. 78–79. As is emphasized by M. Henry, 'social' and 'labor time' were emphasized by Marx.

29 *Capital II*, translated by Moor and Aveling, p. 358.

30 *Capital I*, translated by Moore and Aveling, p. 484.

Index